The Good Life

Cheers

Tom Shepherd

THE GOOD LIFE

*Tom And Too Tall's Triumph
Over the Great Depression and WWII*

TOM SHEPHERD

Two Harbors Press
Minneapolis, MN

Two Harbors Press
212 3rd Avenue North, Suite 290
Minneapolis, MN 55401
612.455.2293
www.TwoHarborsPress.com

ISBN-13: 978-1-936401-36-9
LCCN: 2011920840

Distributed by Itasca Books

Book Design by Sophie Chi

Printed in the United States of America

Dedication

Stephen Spender said, "History is the ship carrying living memories to the future." This book is my effort to pass on recollections of growing up in the '30s and '40s to future generations. I lived them and hope you will enjoy reading them.

My daughter, Rebecca, is the engine that made *The Good Life* possible. She often said, "Dad, I believe I would say it this way, but it's your book." She was always right and always gave me an opportunity to think it over. Rebecca would be worth her weight in gold to any author.

Her daughter-in-law, Kristina, also was an engine that made *The Good Life* turn out just as I dreamed. Two engines pulling for me, and my wife Eunice encouraging me ... how could an eighty-three-year-old have it any better than that?

Thank you from the bottom of my heart, girls!

Preface

Something amazing happened on July 4th, 2008. My wife and I were attending an antique sale when I discovered the very telegraph key I had used sixty-six years ago. This discovery led to the idea of writing down memories from my days working as a telegrapher for the Illinois Central Railroad. After finishing the undertaking, I sent a copy to all my children, thinking it would be a nice keepsake for our family. As a surprise that Christmas I received a copy of all my stories in a beautiful hard-bound book. My daughter and son-in-law even traveled to the cities where I had worked to snap pictures of depots that might be still standing.

After discovering that I enjoyed writing so much, I decided to record other events of my life. Subsequently, it occurred to me that older people who had lived during that time could relate to my experiences and younger people may want to learn what life was like for their parents or grandparents. This book is the result of my endeavor.

My story begins while attending grade school in the 1930s. It continues with the adventures I had growing up with my friend Too Tall during the Great Depression. Times were tough for many people, but, as children, Too Tall and I made do with what we had, enjoyed all of our escapades, and were never actually affected by the difficult financial situation plaguing our country. I continue as a young teenager working as a telegrapher for the Illinois Central Railroad. At seventeen, I enlisted in the U.S. Navy and share my experiences serving in the Philippines during WWII and my safe return home.

There my story ends…for now!

Table of Contents

CHAPTER 1

Ferdinand the Bull

The *Story of Ferdinand*, published in 1936, quickly became a sensation around the world. The book is an imaginative tale of a young bull who would not run and frolic with the other young bulls in the countryside. He preferred to smell the flowers and rest under the trees than fight in bullfights ... until the day when some men and a bumblebee give gentle Ferdinand the opportunity to be ferocious and the most unexpected hero.

The story was adapted by Walt

Disney as a short animated film entitled *Ferdinand the Bull* in 1938.

It was a simple story that offered many lessons to young people. In the classroom, teachers set out jars of onion, apple, oranges, lemons, cinnamon, garlic, and other scents. They taught us that the sense of smell helps us to enjoy life, and the story showed us it is not necessary to follow the crowd.

At the time *The Story of Ferdinand* was popular in America, I was attending Lafayette School in Waterloo and my art teacher discovered that I enjoyed drawing pictures of Ferdinand. One day, she took me aside and asked if I would draw Ferdinand on some invitations for a party she was going to host for the principal and teachers. She needed thirty-five invitations and the school had

no copy machine. In fact, copy machines had not been invented yet! The teacher showed me where to draw the bull on the invitations and said I could work on them during art class. It took me five or six classes to complete the task.

When I finished, I showed the drawings to her and she was very pleased with the results.

My eyes grew very big as she opened her pocketbook and pulled out a dollar bill saying, "I can't thank you enough. You have helped my party to be a real success!"

My heart was pounding. That was the first dollar I had ever earned, and I received it doing something for an adult. I realized at that moment … do something an adult wants done and you can be paid for it.

That one-dollar bill would buy me twenty double-dip ice cream cones, and I earned it doing something I enjoyed!

CHAPTER 2

Pig Tails and Dandelion Greens

When my family moved to our acreage on Ansborough Avenue, the Great Depression was still hanging on. My mother, Emma Marie, continued to work at the Rath Packing Company and was the only one in the family who still had a job. She definitely had her hands full taking care of my stepfather Jerry, who was laid off at the time from the loading dock at Raths, me, my brother, my step-sister Dorothy, and my Uncle Harry, but she was strong and up to the task. Mom was raised on a farm near Elgin, Iowa, and, as a child, she worked in the garden, helped with chores, cooked, baked, and learned how to be self-sufficient from her German mother.

Jerry would spend a large part of the day sharpening her knives. She wore two large, leather belts with pockets that held fifteen to twenty wood-handled knives and they had to be razor-sharp. She also wore steel mesh sleeves on her arms for protection, but she still received cuts on her arms and legs. She showed me the scars and I believe I was the only person to whom she showed them.

Every spring, we purchased one thousand Leghorn roosters from a hatchery for one cent apiece. When the roosters started to get big, the pen looked plumb full of white!

Mother had an extra large cast-iron skillet and could fry two chickens at the same time. When she came home from work and wanted to fry a couple roosters for supper, she would say, "T.J., let's have fried chicken for supper" and I knew what that meant.

I would use my chicken catcher, a wire about ten feet long and bent on the end, hook a rooster by the leg, and pull him up to me. Then I carried the rooster to the back door of the house and waited until Mom was ready. She would bring out two buckets of water, one cold and one hot. I used my jackknife to cut off the head and plunged the rooster into the scalding hot water and then into the cold water so I wouldn't burn my hands. After I plucked off all the feathers, my job was finished, and Mom did the rest. She cooked the fryers in lard rendered from a hog we raised and then butchered. My stepfather, Jerry, killed the hog. I'm not sure how, but I think he shot it and then hung it up in the chicken yard where Mom would do the butchering.

We used almost the entire hog and it was my job to help her clean the guts out. She brought out a teakettle of hot water, and I held the ends of the guts up. Mom poured hot water in and then slid her hands down repeatedly until the guts were clean inside. It took a long time and was hard work. She used the casings for blood sausage. You couldn't get me to eat it, but my German uncles loved it!

I heard my Uncle Harry say, "Emma, you make the best blood sausage I have ever tasted, bar none!"

Mom also boiled the head of the hog, and when it was done, a gelatin-looking substance covered the pieces of meat. She added some spices and made headcheese. The headcheese was chilled and then cut into squares.

Mom would say to me, "Want a piece of headcheese, T.J.?"

"You kidding? Are the eyeballs in that awful looking stuff?"

Mom would laugh and say, "I don't think so, T.J., but thanks for helping me clean out the guts. Your Uncle Adolph is coming to visit this fall. He loves headcheese, but sometimes I think he comes just to see you!"

"I like Uncle Adolph," I replied.

Mom said, "He told me about the slot machine lesson. I really had a good laugh out of that!

In the springtime when the dandelions were in full bloom, Mom would bring tails from the slaughtered hogs home from work. Rath allowed the employees to take hog tails home for free.

After coming home from work, she would say, "T.J., I need some greens."

There was a farm field at the back of our acreage and the fencerows were thick with nice-sized dandelions. I grabbed a bucket (no Wal-Mart sacks in those days) and my jackknife and cut a bucketful of dandelion greens. Our supper menu for that evening was pig tails, dandelion greens, homemade bread with strawberry jam, and bread pudding for dessert with real whipped cream. Mom had to make enough to feed six adults every day. Dorothy, my stepsister, would help, but as soon as she turned eighteen, she moved to Hollywood, Florida, and I never saw her again.

We raised our own ducks and geese and always had a delicious goose for Thanksgiving. The geese were kept in a separate pen because the gander was so mean. My collie, Pat, wasn't afraid of anything except that gander!

Mom always saved the goose grease and strained it into a jar. In the winter when I had a cold or sore throat, she would tear apart wool fabric, rub goose grease over my throat, wrap the wool around my neck, and fasten it with huge safety pins to hold it in place. It worked! I always felt better in the morning.

My collie hated cats and sometimes came home with a dead cat in his mouth to show me. Mom always hated that. He had a long nose, and it was covered with scars from the battles he lost!

One day, Jerry wanted to move a small corn crib we used to store corn for when we raised a hog. We all went out to the crib, including Pat. As it was lifted up, dozens of rats came running out from under the crib. What a sight to see! Pat ran around the crib and killed the rats by snapping their necks. The circle became larger and larger, but he got every one of them.

When I was little, Pat was always by my side. If anyone came too near, he would immediately get between me and whoever was getting too close and growl. I would always say, "Back off or Pat might bite you."

One day after running in the woods in back of our land, he returned home smelling like a skunk

9

and, wow, did he ever stink! Mom made me give him a bath.

During this time, gold buyers were always coming to the door wanting to buy any gold or jewelry you were willing to sell. We returned home one afternoon to find a gold buyer on the front porch. Pat was lying on the ground near the steps. Was that gold buyer ever mad! Pat had allowed him on the front porch, but wouldn't let him off. I laughed and laughed!

The gold buyer yelled, "Shut up, kid, and get that damn dog away from here! I've been here all afternoon."

Mom then told me to take Pat around in back so the man could leave.

Mom always planted a huge garden. I believe it was around an acre and, of course, she had two boys to keep the weeds pulled and harvest the crop. When the peas ripened, it was an all-day job. My brother, Bob, and I would pick a bushel or two and sit on the front porch where it was cooler and husk them out. Mother would then can them in her huge pressure cooker. She also canned green beans, corn, and tomatoes. You name it, we grew it, and Mom canned it!

Canning was done on the weekends so she could supervise the whole operation. We had dozens of shelves in the basement and, by fall, they were filled with jars of vegetables. My

Grandma Friedrichs had taught mom how to survive and it was foolproof. I now understood why we moved to the acreage. We had two acres of land and that was enough to have a large garden and raise chickens and hogs for food in case she lost her job. Our lot on Fowler Street was only about fifty by one hundred feet and after taking out for the house and garage, there was little land left for a garden. Also, being in the city limits did not allow us to raise any animals. Mom never did lose her job during the Depression, but was sure thinking ahead just in case she did.

Mom always had us eat oranges. She said it kept us from getting colds. I wasn't sure about that, but I pounded a row of nails along the floor joists in the basement and hung the peelings. When they were really dry and covered with mold, they were ready to eat. I brushed off the mold (it came off easily when they were good and dry) and that was my dessert. They tasted exceptionally good! My friend we called Too Tall liked them also and sometimes asked me if any of the orange peels were ready to eat.

Every year Mom made a goal to have fried chicken and sweet corn by the Fourth of July, and we usually reached that goal. She liked to plant potatoes by Good Friday, but sometimes Iowa winters made that hard to achieve.

CHAPTER 3

Egg on the Sidewalk

It was freezing cold in the Hog Kill Department and standing in rubber boots all day was painful, but my mother, Emma Marie, worked for twenty years trimming fat off the hog meat. It was a hard and dangerous job. Maybe all the years of hard labor helped her to stay in shape. She lived to be ninety-two years old. Bless her soul!

She was a sharp card player and could remember every card played in a game.

When Mom was eighty-five years old, a friend of mine told me, "Tom, do you know your mother goes to the tavern on LaPorte Road every afternoon and walks out with the young players' money? They say she's a card shark. If one of those guys gets a few draws in him, he might follow her outside and heaven only knows what he might do because of a little money he lost."

"Thanks for telling me, Rick. I'll talk to her and get that stopped."

Mom and I had our conversation, and she promised to quit going to the tavern and playing poker with the young men. She quit as promised, but then started going to the Meskwaki Indian Reservation to play poker. She at least would be safe there, so I thought it would be a good compromise.

One July morning in 1936, Mom woke my brother and me extra early to work in the garden before it got too hot. The temperature was forecast to set a record for the day. It did, and the thermometer climbed to 108 degrees.

Mom commented to us, "It's going to get hot enough to fry eggs on the sidewalk."

After Bob and I finished with the garden work, I raced over to Too Tall's house and told him what Mom had said.

Too Tall excitedly replied, "Let's try it, Tom!"

I was already ahead of him. In my pocket, I was carrying a few eggs. Too Tall and I cracked the eggs on the sidewalk and they fried just fine!

CHAPTER 4

Clyde Miller Rodeo

A short distance from my home on Ansborough Avenue, the Clyde Miller Rodeo would come to town and set up each year. About a quarter mile west of the rodeo site was a large fenced area. The forty or so acres consisted mostly of oak trees with a few acres of pasture. All the horses and Brahma bulls were kept there, and being a quarter mile from the rodeo site, the animals could not be seen from the road. At that time, Ansborough Avenue was a gravel road and also the city limits line for Waterloo, making the rodeo site just outside the city limits.

My friend, Too Tall, and I put on our Indian outfits and sneaked into the pasture with the horses and Brahma bulls. Too Tall grabbed the mane of a buckin' bronco and up he went onto the horse's back.

"Grab a mane, Tom," he yelled to me.

The horses didn't try to buck us off, but just walked around in the woods.

Too Tall said, "Let's try a Brahma bull!"

I hesitated a little, but finally agreed. Holy cow! Those bulls were giants, but we grabbed the hump on their back and pulled ourselves up. We scratched their ears and humps and they loved the special treatment. The bulls' backs were wide so we laid back and took a nap in the afternoon.

I guess you know they are made to buck by tying a leather strap to their private parts. The horses and bulls would buck to try to get the leather strap off. I am sure that must have been painful.

The rodeo built a double fence, each about ten feet from the other, around the rodeo site. A cowboy on a horse rode around and around between the fences to prevent anyone from sneaking in without a ticket. He carried a leather whip, and he meant business!

It was during the Great Depression and Too Tall and I could not afford the price of admission.

"No problem!" I said to Too Tall. "Look at the high bushes on the south end. That will be our way in."

After it got dark, we crawled up into the bushes and waited for the cowboy to ride past. After he rode slowly out of sight, Too Tall and I took turns crawling up to the fence and cutting the wire with a wire cutter. I went first and started to cut a square opening that could be lifted up and then put back down without being detected. Too Tall signaled me when the cowboy was coming, and I crawled back into the bushes. Next, it was Too Tall's turn. He crawled up to the fence and snipped the wire until the hole was large enough to slide through. He then hooked two hog rings on the top so the opening would swing back into place after we got through. We also made a hole in the inner fence. The inner opening was a lot more difficult and took longer, but we got it done.

I whispered to Too Tall, "I'll go first, but be sure to whistle if that cowboy gets too close. I bet that whip would really sting!"

The openings in the fences were near the bleachers and as soon as the cowboy rode past, through the fences we would go and disappear into the crowd.

We watched the bulls buck off the cowboys and laughed knowing we had taken naps on their backs early that afternoon!

The rodeo had a large popcorn machine and did it ever smell good! I approached the popcorn

17

vender and asked if we could have the partial and unpopped corn that fell to the bottom.

"I have a penny for two sacks."

"Give me your penny, kid," he said and filled two sacks.

It was hard chewing, but it was hot and good!

We went to the rodeo every night it was in town and rode the bulls every day. My mom asked me where I was getting the money to buy tickets.

I said, "Kids get in free, Mom."

I should have said, "The Great Depression, penniless kids always find their way in free!"

There is still a Clyde Miller Rodeo in the Midwest. Maybe they still set up in Waterloo, Iowa, but I am sure they don't erect a double fence around the site with a cowboy wielding a leather whip anymore. Kids nowadays have money for tickets.

Side note: Do you know what first broke the sound barrier? It was not an airplane, but the end of a cowboy's leather whip. The cracking sound you hear is the whip breaking the sound barrier.

CHAPTER 5

Summer Indians

As soon as school was out for the summer, Too Tall suggested, "Tom, let's get a Mohawk haircut!"

"Don't you think we should ask our mothers first?" I replied.

We asked and got permission and the money, because we both needed a haircut.

Mom said, "I bet Reverend Deirs will have a stroke when he sees you in church with a Mohawk! Oh well, I know you and Too Tall love to play like Indians all summer. It sounds like a lot of fun."

"Where is that leather notebook you are always writing notes in? Let's make a list of all the supplies we will need," Too Tall said.

When I returned with my notebook, he added, "Gosh, Tom, I just realized we need everything!

First, we will have to make a couple of hunting knives from old files."

"Forget that," I said. "Remember, my mom works on the hog kill, and she is always throwing old knives away. I can get a couple of them. All we need to do is make sheaths."

We roamed the woods along Black Hawk Creek looking for the perfect limbs to make bows and arrows. An old leather coat was found in Too Tall's garage. That was our greatest find of all! We used it to make sheaths for our knives, and pouches to carry matches, our pipes made of reeds and corncobs, fish hooks, and dried cornsilk to smoke. Arrowheads were fashioned from pieces of chipped stone or small sharpened pieces of metal. We painted the stocks on our BB guns red and found a large piece of heavy canvas to make crude bags to carry our equipment. The entire summer was spent searching for materials to make things we needed.

We also wanted to find copper wire, heavy-duty thread, and feathers. We liked Plymouth Rock chicken feathers the best, but they were hard to find. Down the street lived an older lady who was called "Turkey Tom." A lot of weeds grew around her fenced-in turkeys and gave us some cover. I used my wire chicken catcher to hook a turkey by the leg, pull it over to the fence, and pluck out the feathers we wanted before letting the turkey go free.

We had an old frying pan and a tin pan with a handle to dip water from the creek to fill our canteens. Back then, Black Hawk Creek was not polluted. We hid flour, salt, and lard near our favorite fishing hole. I would fish and Too Tall would be on the lookout for older kids roaming the woods looking for trouble. We always caught plenty of Blue Gills and I would clean them in the creek. Fish, wild asparagus, and maybe an apple were a great meal when we were hungry! I kept our fire as low as I could and put it out as soon as we were finished cooking.

Too Tall and I made a pact, lit our pipes, and smoked on them to seal the pact forever.

Our hero was the great Indian, Chief Black Hawk. Our county and the creek where we roamed were named after him. Too Tall and I spent the summer imagining we were Chief Black Hawk warriors!

We learned to walk through the woods as quietly as an Indian. Too Tall and I wanted to spy on the other kids so we could hide or take another trail to avoid them. The woods along Black Hawk Creek were several miles long and there was room for everybody, but some kids looked for trouble and would shoot us with their BB guns or want to fight. One thing was in our favor. We chose a site that was difficult to get to, so we never had any trouble where we fished and cooked. When we got close to town, we took unused trails.

We had a wonderful time all summer long, but fall was closing in on us. Our Mohawk haircuts were growing out, and it was time to get ready to go back to school.

The next spring of 1937, when Too Tall was nine and I was ten, we went swimming in the creek. Huge chunks of ice floated on the water, but we built a fire on shore to keep warm. My older brother, Bob, found out about it and told Mother.

"Did you go swimming in Black Hawk Creek with ice still floating in the water?" she asked. "Don't you know you could have drowned in that ice-cold water? To the basement, Tom."

I knew what that meant. To the basement we went, and I had to drop my pants while mom took hold of my hand. She had a leather razor strap and whacked me good as I ran around in a circle. The leather strap was about three inches wide and really smarted. I didn't cry though, and I think that disturbed Mom a little because the last whack was a good one. My mom's method of punishment isn't recommended, but it worked. I never went swimming in Black Hawk Creek in the early spring again!

CHAPTER 6

Baby Face

In the early 1930s, the police station on West Fifth and Sycamore Street looked like a small library with several concrete steps up to the dilapidated old building. Officer Emil Steffen had just checked in for duty and, at his briefing, was informed that one of the Dillinger gang was in Waterloo, probably casing out banks for a possible robbery.

After the briefing, he left the station to begin his downtown beat. The gangster, Baby Face Nelson, had just come out of a local tavern and spotted Officer Steffen in uniform coming down the steps of what he may have thought was a library. Baby Face panicked, pulled out his pistol, and started running down Sycamore Street. He turned into the first alley, thinking he could lose

Officer Steffen, but it was a dead end. Baby Face was trapped!

Officer Steffen pursued him into the alley and when Baby Face saw him, he raised his pistol, took aim, and shot. Bang! He missed Officer Steffen, but Officer Steffen had the courage to face a gangster in a dark alley and shoot him dead with his revolver!

The incident was written about in the newspaper and Officer Steffen was a hero!

CHAPTER 7

Gypsies

In 1936, just down the street from where I lived, were the railroad tracks for the Interurban Railroad. The railroad ran from Waterloo to Cedar Rapids, Iowa, each day. Just below a large hill called the Viaduct, a tribe of gypsies would set up camp and stay all summer. At least twenty-five people made up the tribe, plus one Queen, who was the ruler. Everything had to be approved by her.

The gypsies, a Caucasian people who originated in India, were known for wandering around the country and stealing anything they could get their hands on, but I had many dealings with them and was always treated fairly. They lived in tents, cooked on open fires, and loved music. Their clothing was made by the women in the tribe, long, pretty dresses and leather vests

25

with dingle-dangles tied on them. They were all quite beautiful with dark skin, long, dark hair tied with ribbons, and rings on almost every finger.

The Queen and some of the young men could speak good English, and I enjoyed talking with them. I think the reason they liked me is because I didn't care about their bad reputation.

Sometimes in the morning when my chores were finished, I took a canvas bag and filled it with carrots, beans, and anything that would not be missed. An acre of garden produced a lot of vegetables. I would also catch two Leghorn roosters and take off for the gypsy camp. I suppose they probably paid me very little for it all, but I didn't care because the Queen always had me stay for lunch. The food they cooked on open fires in cast iron cookware was delicious. One of the young gypsy girls would come and sit by me, but because of my age, I wasn't interested in girls and didn't pay much attention to her. Whenever I went after dark and they were playing their musical instruments, we would dance together.

The gypsies I knew were really hard working people. They had a business building chairs and furniture from willow branches. Each morning all the able-bodied men and women would meet at the Queen's tent to get their orders and discuss the day's work. They divided up into three groups. One group would go out along the river to collect willow branches. Another group, the largest, stayed at the camp and made the furniture. The third group put on nice, clean clothes, loaded a truck with furniture, and traveled all over Black Hawk County trying to sell it.

In the fall of the year, as soon as it began to get cold, the Queen made the decision to pack up and leave for a campground where the weather was warmer. Maybe they could be called the original snowbirds!

One year the gypsies purchased some inexpensive ground in our county and built some houses. The willow chair business could not sustain them, so they went into the asphalting business. They purchased large trucks and other equipment and were very successful. I believe they are still in the blacktopping business today.

CHAPTER 8

Diving Helmet

One Indian summer evening, Too Tall and I were enjoying some licorice sticks I had purchased at Kat's Supermarket on Falls Avenue. They were really long and the ridges that twirled around the sticks were nice and thick. We always chewed off the ridges first and then ate the licorice stick.

We learned to make things last in the Great Depression. My collie dog, Pat, was watching me like a hawk, because he knew I would treat him to the last bite of licorice and, of course, Too Tall would do the same.

"Hey, Too Tall," I said. "I have to tell you a good one! My mom just had a new sidearm hot water heater installed in the basement beside the furnace, because the old sidearm was damaged."

Too Tall didn't have a basement or sidearm heater, so I explained that in winter, the furnace would heat the water in the sidearm, but in the summer when the furnace wasn't on, a gas burner had to be lit with a match. Then the gas burner would be turned off once the water was hot.

"You can't repeat this, because my mom doesn't want anyone to know, but one Sunday we went to visit my grandmother in Elgin, Iowa, and returned home in the late afternoon. Jerry, my step-dad, wanted to use the bathroom first. He had forgotten to turn off the gas burner before we left and flushed the toilet while still seated. He will never forget to turn off the gas burner again! The entire water system had turned to steam and burned his butt really bad. He couldn't sit down for a month!"

"You know what?" I added. "I was looking at a *Life* magazine and saw pictures of a U.S. Navy diving helmet and thought, I bet we could make a diving helmet out of that old sidearm heater."

"A diving helmet?" Too Tall asked.

"Yes, a diving helmet. I have a plan in my head already, and when we are finished making the helmet, we could take it to Clear Lake and try it out. We'll get rich finding sunken boats, outboard motors, and maybe sunken treasure at the bottom of the lake!"

"Wow!" said Too Tall. "I've never been rich before."

"I'll get my leather notebook and draw a plan on how to build it. I know my mom won't care if we take the old heater. They dumped it out behind the chicken coop."

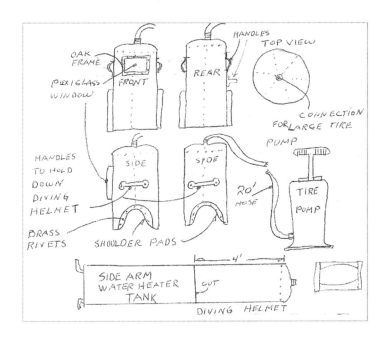

I showed him the list of things we would need.

"The most costly item will be a truck tire pump. We'll also need a piece of Plexiglas for the window, some brass bolts, and a long length of rubber hose to connect from the pump to the top of the helmet."

Too Tall looked at the list and said, "My brother has an old heavy-duty truck tire pump in the garage. I know he'll let us have it. It probably needs new washers or something, but I bet we can repair it."

"Great!" I said. "We'll also need a couple of handles, some oak for the window, and some leather to make the shoulder pads. It shouldn't be too hard to gather up the things we need."

So we sawed and drilled, riveted and filed, sawed and drilled some more, but, by golly, we got our diving helmet built! Now all we needed was to get to Clear Lake.

"You know my friend Walter who lives on Byron Avenue? He goes fishing with his dad at Clear Lake all the time. I'll show him the helmet and see if he will ask his dad to take us along next time," I said.

They were going fishing the next weekend and agreed to take us along. Too Tall and I were thrilled to death, because we still thought that if our diving helmet worked like we knew it would, maybe we could get rich. I don't think we really understood what being rich meant. We thought getting a hundred dollars would make a person rich.

When Mr. Donahue and Walter pulled up, we put all of our gear and the diving helmet in the boat and jumped in the car. Too Tall and I were just bursting with excitement to think we had made a diving helmet and were on our way to try it out in Clear Lake!

After arriving at the lake, we launched the boat and Mr. Donahue took us out to where the water was about ten feet deep. Then we lowered the anchor. There was no wind and a perfect time to try out our "get-rich-quick" diving helmet. I asked Too Tall if he wanted to try it out first.

"No, Tom. I'm a little scared."

"OK, I'll go first. When I get on the helmet and down in the water, don't stop pumping the truck pump for anything, because the water level will come up in the helmet."

Down I went, and Too Tall started pumping his heart out! He didn't want anything to happen to me.

The diving helmet worked perfectly. Pumping air into the helmet kept the water level below the Plexiglas window, and I could see around the bottom of the lake, but the air from the rubber hose was so pungent I could hardly breathe it. I started to feel a little nauseated, so I ducked under the helmet and swam up to the boat.

I told Too Tall what had happened and he said, "Oh, Tom, did I pump hard enough?"

"You did fine. I just couldn't breathe the pungent, rubber-smelling air," I explained. "Would you like to try it?"

"No, I'm too scared."

"I don't blame you, Too Tall, but we had a great time building our diving helmet and it did work as we planned."

We thoroughly enjoyed our trip to Clear Lake, and after returning to Waterloo, Mr. Donahue dropped us each off at our homes. We thanked him and he said, "You boys built a great diving helmet and it worked! You should be proud."

We both got out of the car, but forgot to take the diving helmet out of the boat. It had been a long day and I guess we were tired. A few months later the Donahue family moved to Minneapolis, Minnesota, and must have taken our diving helmet with them.

After Too Tall and I grew up, we lost track of the helmet and actually never thought about it again. Believe it or not, years later, an ocean- and water-themed display case was exhibited at the Mall of America in Minneapolis, Minnesota. In a glass case were several diving helmets. On the far left, a sign read: HOMEMADE DIVING HELMET and it was ours! It was made from a sidearm heater with brass bolts, an oak frame around a Plexiglas window with leather shoulder pads. It was wonderful to see our diving helmet again!

I don't know for sure how our helmet happened to be in the Mall of America's display, but since the Donahues took our helmet with them when they moved to Minneapolis, that had to be the connection. I bet Too Tall would be amazed if he knew where our "get-rich-quick" idea for a diving helmet ended up! So our accomplishment is still alive and entertaining children at the Mall of America. Maybe a couple of kids like us will see what we did with a sidearm heater and say, "Let's design and build something! Maybe it will make us rich!"

Eventually, Too Tall became a schoolteacher in the state of Washington, and I worked for the Waterloo Fire Department as a firefighter for thirty-two years.

CHAPTER 9

Edison School

In 1935 we lived on Fowler Street in Waterloo, Iowa, and a streetcar ran from Fowler Street to downtown Waterloo. A pole with a wheel on the rear of the car touched an overhead charged electrical wire and passed the charge down to the motor. If the streetcar was going to stop for any length of time, the conductor could pull the pole off the live wire with an attached rope. There was one thing wrong with that system! No, I never pulled this trick on the conductor, but kids would hide in the bushes and when the streetcar passed, especially on a hill, they ran out, pulled the pole off the wire, and the car would stop. I bet the conductors got angry, especially in the cold wintertime, because they had to get out of the streetcar and reattach the wheel to the line.

As the conductor trolled down the street, he rang a brass bell to let people know he was coming. I think the ride downtown cost only five cents for a child.

Many of the neighborhoods in Waterloo at that time had an alley at the back of the lot. Almost every week, a Jewish man came down the alley riding on the spring seat in the front of his horse-drawn wagon. He had a long beard and dressed in a black suit with a black felt hat. He rang a bell to let you know he was coming. He would purchase almost anything you wanted to sell … old iron, tin, wire, jewelry, and even gold. Times were hard, and sometimes people had to sell even keepsakes just to get by. In the fall, kids threw rotten tomatoes at him, but he acted like he didn't mind. I guess you could say that Jewish fellow had the last laugh. Kats was the family name, and they became rich selling scrap metal needed for the war effort during World War II.

It seemed everyone in my east side neighborhood were poor as a church mouse. If someone in the neighborhood got married, the kids would have a shivaree after dark. They would bang pots and pans together and yell half of the night. Many newlyweds had to live with the bride's or groom's parents.

Many of the houses, especially the basements, smelled like home-brewed beer. If the caps were not attached tightly enough, they would explode and out ran the foaming beer. The smell would permeate the basement and eventually the entire house.

When we moved from Fowler Street to the acreage on Ansborough Avenue, I had to transfer to Edison School. It was about six blocks away from our new home and within walking distance. The first day at my new school, I learned some valuable lessons. The principal called me into his office and, after asking a lot of questions, went over the school rules with me.

If the teacher caught you breaking a rule, like running in the halls or not paying attention in class, he or she would call a monitor. All the monitors had a paddle with randomly spaced holes drilled in them. The misbehaving student had to bend over, grab his ankles, and the monitors would smack the offender's bottom as many times as the teacher thought he needed. The monitors were mean, older kids, and I decided I wasn't going to do anything wrong and get whacked with one of their paddles. I talked to another student one time, and he said the holes in the paddles left blisters!

My English teacher was very mean, and everyone disliked her. I believe she thought her English class was a reform school! Reform schools were like prisons for teenagers back in the 1930s.

I made friends at my new school with a student named Cecil Deeds. He was a tough kid and hated school. One day he did something wrong in English class, and the teacher ordered a monitor to hit Cecil on the butt five times and send him home. The next day in class, the teacher called on Cecil to answer a question she knew he would not be able to answer. That was mean, but Cecil walked up to her desk and hit her in the mouth with his fist. Her face quickly covered with blood. She screamed, slumped down in her chair, and began to cry. That was the end of Cecil Deeds' education! I never saw him in school again and wondered how many whacks he would have gotten for hitting a teacher in the mouth. It would probably take all day.

In the 1930s, I was always looking for a way to make a little money. I had never heard of an allowance during the Great Depression, but I had a marble in my pocket that rolled almost perfectly. Back then, we called a perfectly balanced marble a steely. It was called a steely because it made you money. It reminded me of the saying "It's like stealing candy from a baby."

I practiced for hours and hours rolling my steely into a hole until I hardly missed. On the school grounds or behind the baseball stadium was a good place to find kids with a marble and some change in their pockets. I would make a small hole in the ground with my pocketknife and draw a line in the dirt about ten feet away. Then I tossed a penny or nickel into the hole. The person who was able to roll their marble into the hole from the line won the money. I had to be careful, though, because some of the older kids were poor losers.

On the corner across the street from the school, a man had an enclosed front porch and sold candy to school kids. His biggest attraction, though, was punch boards. They worked similar to slot machines. The tiny slips of paper you punched out mostly got you nothing, but sometimes we won chocolate marshmallow cups. I loved chocolate marshmallow cups, so the punch cards were a seductive draw. I think I was one of his best customers, because I spent a lot of the money I earned on punch cards.

Edison School was a well-built, brick building with a large playground. In the summer, the school system would hire female students from the State Teacher's College in Cedar Falls to supervise all the playgrounds at the schools. They brought a huge, padlocked box full of footballs, basketballs, and any equipment that was useful for keeping kids busy.

The student teacher at Edison School that summer was a really cute blonde. At a certain time in the afternoon, stories were read to the

41

kids. She always sat on the top step in front of the door of the school on the playground side while the children sat on the steps below or on the ground. All of the boys, and I mean *all* the boys, in the neighborhood never missed story reading time. Why? The student teacher sat on the top step wearing a skirt, but no panties. If the superintendent of the schools would have found out, I wonder how many whacks she would have gotten with one of those Edison paddles with the holes drilled in them!

CHAPTER 10

Amazing Uncle Adolph

The Friedrichs family immigrated to America from Langen, Germany. The port of departure was Hamburg, Germany, and the destination was Postville, Iowa. They arrived at Ellis Island on March 11, 1904 on the ship *Graf Waldersee*. The ship's roster included Adolf Friedrichs, age thirty-six, Helene, age thirty-seven, Adolph, age nine, Minnie, age eight, Wilhelm, age four, and Hans, age one year and six months. My Uncle Harry and my mother, Emma, were both born after the family settled in America. Two brothers were left in Germany, because they were over fourteen years old. At that time, no male over fourteen was allowed to leave

Germany, because they could be drafted into the army.

The family bought a farm near Elgin, Iowa. After a few years, tragedy struck. Grandfather Friedrichs had taken a farm wagon and a team of horses to Sumner to buy supplies. On the way back to the farm, he was run over by the farm wagon and killed. No one knows what happened or how it happened, because Grandpa Friedrichs was alone. A set of child's play dishes he had purchased for my mother, Emma, were found near the wagon. Because Uncle Adolph was the oldest son, he had to take charge of the family farm.

Eventually all the children left the farm and went out on their own. Grandma then sold the farm, moved into town, and bought a small house across the street from the Del Monte Canning Factory.

Grandma Friedrichs spoke mostly German and could speak only a few words of English. I always enjoyed listening to her speak in her native tongue.

I remember my brother, Bob, and I would help her work in the large garden behind the house. Outside near the back door, sat a large wooden barrel. A rock sat on the lid to hold it in place. Yes, she was making a barrel of sauerkraut. Every time I went out the door, I would take off

The Friedrichs family

Tom is standing in the front row to the left

the lid, reach in, and grab a handful. I really liked it, and Grandma Friedrichs didn't mind.

A building in the backyard that looked like a small garage served as an icehouse. In the winter, men would saw blocks of ice from the Turkey River and place them in the icehouse with saw dust between each layer until the icehouse was full. It would last all summer. When Grandma needed some ice, she would send Bob and me out to get it. We thought that was fun, because it was nice and cool in the icehouse. In the summer, she made us fresh lemonade with chipped ice. It was very refreshing on a hot day.

When I was in the Navy, Grandma sent me a birthday card and I wrote her a letter dated October 25, 1945. She passed away while I was serving in the U.S. Navy in the South Pacific. I cried when I received the news. I loved my Grandma Friedrichs.

Uncle Adolph was the greatest and most intelligent person I have ever known. He had only a fourth-grade education in Germany, but he studied on his own and became an electrical engineer. I always wished I had been old enough to work with him and learn from him. He designed and supervised the building of dams and electrical power stations on the Turkey, Volga, and Wapsipinicon Rivers running through small towns like Postville and Elkader in northeast

Iowa. What a great achievement for an immigrant from Germany with a fourth-grade education!

Eventually, Uncle Adolph moved to Williamsfield, Illinois, and owned and operated an electrical power company in the area. He owned everything needed to operate his business, even the light poles, but he purchased the electricity from a large power company in Peoria.

Uncle Adolph had an office in downtown Williamsfield, and his wife, Signa, worked in the office. They also sold small electric appliances like toasters.

My first summer spent with Uncle Adolph was absolutely a dream vacation for a ten-year-old! Two o'clock in the afternoon was the time. The Rite Spot Tavern was the place. I had to be there on time to get a root beer soda, and Uncle Adolph would have a draw. Of course, I realized in later years that was his way of keeping track of me.

In the late 1930s, all the fields from Williamsfield to Peoria were farms. At threshing time, the farmers would get together and help each other. The threshing machines would be belching out smoke and making a lot of noise. It seemed to me everyone had a good time working together. The farm wives brought every kind of delicious food imaginable, and the young girls dished it out. They wore cute bonnets and were always laughing or giggling. My friend and I would just get in line at mealtime and no one seemed to mind.

I really enjoyed going with Uncle Adolph to check power lines and do routine maintenance on the electrical system. One hot summer day, we were driving down a gravel road and Uncle Adolph said to me, "Tommy, look down the road. There's a tornado coming our way!"

It had a huge funnel and the end on the ground was twisting back and forth. Uncle Adolph made a U-turn, and down the road we went as fast as that 1935 Ford pickup would go! Luck was with us, because we were able to outrun that huge tornado.

We stopped for lunch at a small restaurant out in the country. In the 1930s, slot machines were legal in Illinois. Uncle Adolph was going to teach me a lesson, so he gave me a dime to put in the slot machine and said, "Put in your dime, Tommy, and pull the lever. Those slot machines just gobble up your money."

I pulled the lever, and, wow, I hit the jackpot and collected five dollars worth of dimes. That was a fortune to me! Uncle Adolph could hardly wait to tell my mom about the lesson he was going to teach me and how it backfired!

One day we went out to check power lines together and drove past a house in a rural area around Williamsfield.

Uncle Adolph said, "Tommy, look at that new Lincoln Zephyr in the driveway. They never pay their electric bill on time, and now they have a brand new car."

We continued down the road and Uncle Adolph spotted a transformer that didn't look right to him, so he decided to check it out. He put on his climbing gear and went up the pole. When he opened the door of the transformer, it exploded in his face. I thought it had killed him. Boy, was I scared! A pickup truck was coming down the country road and I ran out into the street waving my arms and yelling. I begged the two farmers to please help my uncle. They knew Uncle Adolph. Most everybody in the county knew my Uncle Adolph. The farmers helped get him down the pole. I don't remember exactly how, but they got him to the ground. The electrical charge that hit him in the face caused the blood vessels to stand out on his chin and cheeks. I always wished I had the same thing on my face, because I thought it looked really cool!

Everyone looked forward to Friday nights. We would drive to a tavern in some small town near Williamsfield and have whole catfish cooked with cornmeal. Of course, all the adults would also have a beer.

Uncle Adolph knew Laurence Welk, the bandleader. He would book him for the dance halls around Williamsfield. My Uncle Adolph loved to dance and continued to dance until he was very old.

He always said to me, "Dancing is good exercise, Tommy."

I must have believed him, because I still do a little dancing at the age of eighty-three.

CHAPTER 11

Cast Iron Chicken Fryer

Mother was working on the hog kill everyday at Rath Packing Company, but she would still oversee all the activity on our acreage. We planted a large garden, raised chickens, geese, ducks, and also a hog. Mom grew just about anything the nurseries could think up to raise in a garden! My brother, Bob, and my responsibility was to keep the weeds hoed out of the garden, and if the peas or green beans were ripe, we picked them so Mom could can them.

My stepfather, Jerry, was laid off from Rath at the time, so was always home to supervise our work. He treated my brother and me poorly while our mother was at work. It was mostly petty things, like making me hoe left-handed, but it made my brother furious whenever Jerry picked on me. Being three years older, Bob always tried to protect me, and I looked up to him for it.

One summer day, Bob took me aside and told me about a plan he had to stop Jerry from ever picking on us again. He would set Mom's huge cast iron chicken fryer on the corner of the table and place one of the chairs nearby.

"I will call Jerry into the kitchen, and when he reaches the right spot, I will grab his arms and hold them. Your job, Tommy, is to jump up on the chair, grab the skillet and hit him over the head," he explained.

It didn't take long until the time was right to execute our plan. Bob called Jerry into the kitchen, grabbed his arms, and held them tight. I jumped up on the chair, picked up the cast iron skillet, and with all the strength I had, hit him over the head. The frying pan broke right down the middle and landed on the kitchen floor. It really scared me. I jumped down off the chair and ran out of the house as fast as I could. If Jerry caught me, I would get a good beating. I never looked back until I reached Cedar Falls, some seven miles from our house, and hid somewhere I knew would be safe. When it came time for Mother to return from work, I headed home. Mom ruled the house and I knew she would not allow Jerry to beat me for hitting him over the head.

As I approached the house, I met my brother and asked him what happened when Mother got home.

The author with his Stepfather, Jerry, and his brother, Bob

"Well, Tommy," he said, "Jerry got a nice-sized lump on his head, but I told him if he picks on you anymore, we would kill him next time, and if he says anything to Mom, I would show her where he hides his whiskey in the garage."

Not a word was said to Mom and Jerry made up some excuse as to how the skillet was broken in two.

Bob laughed and laughed, and Jerry never picked on me again. I am sure he knew my brother meant business!

CHAPTER 12

Cream Puffs

"Hey, Too Tall! I have another idea to make some spending money," I announced.

Too Tall was my best buddy; his real name was Richie Nelson. He was a year younger than me and a little taller, so I called him Too Tall. He liked that moniker because when we had any dealings with adults, they always assumed he was the same age as me and he liked that!

*Too Tall, Tom,
and Pat (the dog)*

55

"Yesterday I went to the Rath Packing Company office with my mother," I told him.

Rath Packing Company front office,
photo credit: Historic American
Engineering Record (Library of Congress),
HAER IOWA,7-WATLO,4E-2

The office, a large two-story building with several concrete steps leading up to the front door, was located across the street from the plant.

"I don't know why she had to go there, but it probably had something to do with her paycheck. We were early for her appointment, so she decided to take me across the street to tour the hog and cattle killing departments that the public never got to see. I guess she wanted me to know what the animals went through when they were slaughtered. It was a horrible thing for me to see," I told Too Tall. "Take a deep breath and, if you like, I'll tell you what I saw."

"Go ahead," Tom. "If I can't take it I'll let you know and you can stop."

"Well, in the hog kill department, there were two overhead conveyers and workers hooked a chain on the rear leg of the hogs. The conveyers took them to the killing room and a butcher stood on a wooden platform about four feet square. As the squealing, upside down hogs passed by, he stuck a knife in their throat and the blood just spewed out. Then he had to quickly turn and cut the hog's throat on the other side of the conveyer. The butcher stood on a platform, because the blood was deep and ran down into a drain. He also became covered with blood. The butchers traded off every hour, because that is all the killing they could stand. After the hogs' throats were cut, the conveyer went up a story and the hogs were dropped into a tank of hot rosin. As the hog was pulled through the rosin, it removed the hair from the skin. They were immediately cut up by workers and the parts put on a conveyer belt and moved to another cold room. That is where Mom works, cutting the excess fat off the meat. She is paid by the bucket. Are you sick yet, Too Tall?" I asked.

"I'm OK, Tom, but I never want to work at Rath. That's for sure!"

"Do you want to hear how they slaughter the cattle?"

"Go ahead. I can take it."

"OK, but if you want me to stop, let me know. I don't want you to get sick on me! They ran the steers into a pen that had concrete walls. It held about twenty steers at a time. They were crowded in so tightly, they would raise their heads up for air. A worker stood on a platform about two feet above the steers. He had a narrow-headed sledgehammer and as the steers raised their heads, he hit them in the forehead between the eyes and they collapsed to the floor. It is a difficult job and sometimes he missed and hit the steer in the eye. That was a horrible sight to see. When the steers were all lying in a pile on the floor, the concrete wall was raised and the steers would tumble out of the killing room where workers were waiting to hook a chain on their legs. Then they were lifted up and the butchers cut their throats and started the butchering process. Want to hear how they got the sheep into the slaughterhouse? A black billy goat is trained to lead the sheep into the slaughtering area and then he turns and goes down a ramp to lead more to slaughter. Well, Too Tall, after hearing this, I have a feeling you will study hard at school, get a good education, and never apply for a job at the Rath Packing Company!

"Mom then went inside the office and I asked if I could wait outside because it was a peach of a day. There was a NO SMOKING sign on the door and I noticed all kinds of big shots, dressed in fine suits, coming up the steps. They would stick their just-lit cigars and cigarettes in a container filled with fine sand before entering the building. Want to hear my new plan?" I asked Too Tall.

"Tom, I know it will work, whatever you have figured out to do. Do you know the Alstadt and Langlas Day Old Bakery Shop just down the block?"

"Geez, Too Tall, you have guessed part of my new plan already! If it works, we can buy four cream puffs for lunch. They are a little damaged, but are huge and have whipped cream inside. Are you ready for the rest of my plan?"

59

"If it gets me a couple of those cream puffs, just tell me what you want me to do."

"Okie, dokie," I said. "We will need an empty cigar box and some tissue paper. Our jackknives have to be good and sharp and I think we should dress in our Sunday clothes."

"How come?" Too Tall asked.

"Well, we are going to sell cut-off cigars and cigarettes to the big shots coming in and out of the Rath office building. You know, Too Tall, I heard we are in a Depression, whatever that is, and I guess everyone is looking for a bargain. We'll collect all the hardly smoked cigars, especially the ones with the band still on them because they look nicer, trim them up and lay them on the tissue in the cigar box. We'll also trim the cigarettes a little. I figure the cigars will sell for a nickel and a good cigarette for a penny. When I was sitting on the steps in front of the office waiting for my mom, a fancy-dressed dude threw an empty Camel cigarette package at the cigar container and missed. I picked it up, studied it a bit, and noticed the camel in the package must be a female. Just for the fun of it, I cut off part of the tail and made the camel on the package into a male. It was easy to do. I carefully slid off the cellophane wrapper, cut off part of the tail with my jackknife, and applied it in the correct place on the camel. I used a little spit so it would stay in the right place and then carefully put the wrapper back on again. It looked real sharp, and what a great novelty! I bet one of those big shots will pay us for one of them. You game to try my plan? If it is a nice sunny day, we could try it tomorrow. Hey, Too Tall! Your dad smokes cigars. Could you get an empty cigar box? I believe my Uncle Harry smokes Camels. He puts them in a silver case and throws away the package."

We gathered up everything we needed with no trouble: a cigar box, two empty Camel cigarette packages, and I found a clean, white handkerchief to line the cigar box. We placed the trimmed cigars on the handkerchief to make them look nice, took the two cigarette packages and carefully changed the camels into males. We then got on our bikes, pedaled the two or three miles to the Rath office building and immediately checked the cigar disposal container. What luck! There were two nice long cigars, one short cigar, and several nice-size cigarettes. We trimmed them up nicely and placed them on the handkerchief in the cigar box. I tried to sell them right away, but no one bought them. I soon figured out the older men were not interested. They probably had money to buy new cigars, but the younger dudes were interested. I sold two cigars and three cigarettes to young men. We now had thirteen cents, but needed more. I showed a young salesman a Camel

61

package and said, "Sir, you could have a great time showing the male camel to your buddies or even to your girl friend." He liked the idea and handed me a nickel.

"Take it, kid. That's all I'll pay."

I took his nickel and handed him the Camel package. We now had eighteen cents.

I said to Too Tall, "I'm hungry. Let's head to the day old store and buy those four cream puffs for lunch."

Too Tall said, "We need twenty cents and we only have eighteen."

" I'll bet you I can buy four cream puffs for eighteen cents."

We biked to the day old store and spied some damaged cream puffs in an iced case. I said, "Ma'am, we have eighteen cents and would like four cream puffs. The one in the corner has more damage than the others."

"OK, kid. Let me see your eighteen cents."

"Gee whiz, Tom. You sure know how to deal with adults!" exclaimed Too Tall.

Out the door we went with our four cream puffs. On the corner was a bench for people waiting for the streetcar, so we sat down and enjoyed our lunch. I think they were the most delicious cream puffs money could buy! Even Too Tall said, "Tom. Are we in heaven?"

Too Tall eventually went to the Teacher's College in Cedar Falls, Iowa (now named the University of Northern Iowa) and became a teacher in the state of Washington. I was proud of him for getting a good education on his own. I hoped that all the daring and adventuresome things we did as kids helped him to excel and further his education.

CHAPTER 13

Paramount Theater

The Paramount Theater in Waterloo, Iowa, was a magnificent showplace and truly the best in all of Black Hawk County. Its beauty was almost beyond description. The building was constructed of reinforced concrete, brick, and stone. The ceiling was over thirty feet high with lights on a timer that would twinkle and blink like stars. The theater had a huge balcony and above the balcony was the projection room. In the lavish entry hung posters in glass cases advertising future movies and all the top actors. Opulence was everywhere!

The Paramount had the largest stage in the Midwest at the time with a large and impressive velvet motor-driven curtain.

Before each movie, an organ rose slowly up from the basement and played the wonderful songs of the 1930s.

The Woman's and Men's Lounges were in the basement. The Men's Lounge had eight coin-operated telephones and several soft leather chairs where the men could sit and enjoy a cigar.

All you needed to enter was a Buffalo head nickel. I believe every kid in Black Hawk County came to the theater on Kids' Day. On this day, there was a talent show instead of a movie. If you thought you could sing or dance or had any kind of act, you were allowed to go on stage and try your luck. The audience showed no consideration for the actors and would boo and laugh and carry on. Worse yet, a theater employee had a large hook on a long pole. If the audience booed, the performer was hooked around the waist and pulled off the stage. It was a lot of fun! Alstadt and Langlas Bakery gave each child a miniature loaf of bread, and other companies furnished drinks and hot dogs.

Around 1939, my good buddy, Too Tall, said to me, "Tom, did you notice the new candy machine when we went to the movie starring Alice Fay?"

"Yes, I did and I bet you are thinking the same thing I'm thinking."

We had figured out a way to trip the peanut machine. We drilled a hole in a penny and attached a copper wire to the penny. After inserting the penny, pushing the lever back and forth, and getting a handful of peanuts, we pulled on the wire to retrieve our penny. Why couldn't we find a way to trip the new candy machine?

"Holy cow, Too Tall! Did you see that row of Babe Ruths in the candy machine?"

"I sure did and wish I had a nickel to buy one. That's my favorite candy bar."

The candy machine was bolted to the wall so it couldn't be shaken. We had to figure out a way to trip the row of Babe Ruths.

During one of our visits to the theater, I went down to the Men's Lounge and noticed a man using the telephone. The number he called was busy, so he hung up and out came his dime.

One day I had a brainstorm and wondered if I stuffed toilet paper up in the coin return, it would prevent the dime from coming out.

"You with me, Too Tall?" I asked.

"I sure am, Tom. The toilet paper should stop the dime from coming out and the fellow using the phone would be in a hurry to get back to the movie and maybe leave without worrying about his dime."

We hopped on a bus, rode downtown to the theater, and purchased one ticket. Too Tall would go up the fire escape in the alley and I would go up to the balcony and open the door for him. There was no alarm on the door in those days, so it was easy to do. Then we went directly to the candy machine.

"Look, Too Tall! There is a small gap along the edge of the candy machine. I bet I can make a device from some strap iron to trip the Babe Ruths. Now let's go down to the Men's Lounge and stuff toilet paper in all the telephone coin returns before we leave."

Our candy machine tripper was made from an eight-inch piece of strap iron that was three-fourths of an inch wide. We cut a hook on the end and then filed it real smooth. The opening along the side of the candy machine was a design mistake. The next time we went to a movie, we walked to the candy machine, slid our tool in the opening, and hooked onto the wire holding a row of Babe Ruths. I pulled the wire just a little and down came six candy bars! We each stuffed three Babe Ruths in our pockets and headed for the Men's Lounge. No one was in the room, so I said to Too Tall, "Pull out the toilet paper. Let's see what happens."

The paper was gone at the first telephone. The second one yielded four dimes. The third, fourth, fifth, sixth, seventh, and eighth phones produced nine more dimes. Six Babe Ruths and $1.30! What a haul in the Great Depression!

"What's the matter?" I asked Too Tall.

"I feel a little guilty. Are we going to get in trouble, Tom?"

"You know, Too Tall, we are doing a favor for the candy machine makers. They need to improve their design and make them trip-proof. And the AT&T engineers should be kicked in the butt for not designing a fool-proof coin return on the telephones."

I think we taught those engineers a lesson. Now a lever has to be pulled down to get your coin returned and there is no way to stop the coins with paper.

I told Too Tall, "Well, we showed it could be done, but I think we shouldn't trip any more candy and leave the peanut machine alone. One time is enough. I guess it would be considered stealing and we don't want to get in trouble."

"Oh, Tom, I feel better now that you said that. I sure hate to give up those dimes, but I guess we had better!"

A week or so later, Too Tall and I were coming down the hall after a movie. The manager stopped me and said, "I want to talk to you, kid. Is your name Tom Shepherd?"

I told Too Tall to go on home. "I'll talk to you tomorrow." I thought there was going to be some trouble and I didn't want to get Too Tall involved.

The manager was a nice looking young woman and said to come into her office. "Sit down, Tom. I have heard a lot of stories about how you know all the tricks, tripping the candy machine and sneaking into the theater. I need a new head usher who can help me stop all the pilfering that is going on around here, someone like you who knows all the ropes."

"Ma'am, where did you hear that I know all the ropes?"

"I'm not at liberty to tell you that, Tom, but I really need someone like you to help manage this theater. I'm afraid for my job if I don't run a tight ship."

"How much will the job pay?"

"There are twelve usherettes that you will be in charge of. The pay is twenty-five cents an hour."

I told her I would need thirty cents an hour for all that responsibility.

"OK, Tom, but I need results. I will be watching you closely to see how you handle the head usher's job. Here is a list of all your duties and the names of the usherettes. You will absolutely have to be here Saturday afternoon when Kids' Day is over. We have to practice a fire drill. Your job will be to go on stage and give this short speech: "Ladies and gentlemen: there is a fire in the vicinity of the theater and we feel it is best for all to leave calmly by the nearest exit. Thank you."

Head Usher

I had to practice the speech every Saturday on stage. I didn't mind though. I was getting thirty cents an hour for doing it!

When I saw Too Tall again, I asked if he knew how the manager got my name. "I didn't tell anyone, Tom." I believed him and knew he would never tell about any of our doings to the manager.

"Don't faint, Too Tall, but the manager, Sally Reed, hired me to be head usher and my pay will be thirty cents an hour! I asked her if I could hire you as my assistant." But she said, "I can't afford it, Tom. You are already getting all I can afford to pay for a head usher."

To this day, I never found out who told Sally Reed about me.

What a dream job! In charge of twelve nice young girls all around my age and getting thirty cents an hour to boot!

I was given a written list of all my duties as head usher and a list of the duties of the usherettes. It wasn't hard since the girls already knew their responsibilities, so I tried to think up new ideas to help increase the profit for the theater. I wrote down all the new things I intended to implement and new duties for the usherettes. "When you are not busy, check the balcony fire exits. If anyone is hanging around, come and get me. If they are adults, I will call the police department. Always pay attention to the candy and peanut machines. If you see something that doesn't look right, let me know."

I told the employee selling movie tickets, "If you sell only one ticket to a youngster, point him out to me, and if he heads for the balcony, I will follow him." That stopped most of the sneaking in while I was on duty.

My other duties included checking the usherettes' uniforms to make sure they were clean when they came on duty. I always looked over the building and made a note of anything that needed to be cleaned. The employees that cleaned the inside of the theater weren't happy, but after about a month, the manager noticed how clean and shiny everything was looking and told me so.

"Tom, come into my office," she said. "You are doing a wonderful job as head usher. All the girls like you because you never bully them like the last usher did. Thank you so much for working so hard."

I liked my job as head usher, but I was getting older and the economy was changing fast. World War II was starting and played out the Great Depression. I gave my manager a few weeks' notice and explained that there were good jobs opening up everywhere.

"I understand, Tom. Thank you for helping me to get this theater running smoothly again. My superiors noticed all the changes."

I had to tell the usherettes goodbye. That was hard and some of them cried. I bet they would always remember the good time we had working together. It would be wonderful if some of them are still around and live in Waterloo. They would be grandmas or great-grandmas by now, but if they happen to read this book, they will smile from ear to ear knowing Tom is still alive and thinking about them.

In the 1970s, the city decided to demolish the grand old theater. There was a movement to save the building, but it would have cost millions of dollars. The city took bids for the demolition and a company was awarded the job. The theater was built like the Rock of Gibraltar and all the steel in the concrete was too much for their equipment. The company ended up filing for bankruptcy. Another bid was accepted, and the demolition was finished. It was a sad day when the last load of concrete and steel was hauled away.

CHAPTER 14

Canfield Airport

Around 1936, a famous pilot named Colonel Rosco Turner landed on a grass landing strip about five miles east of Waterloo on Highway 20 and was giving rides in his Ford Tri-motor airplane. He was barnstorming all over the country, and later, was the first pilot to fly for an airline with paid passengers.

Mother was very excited about the prospect of a plane ride so we went over to the airstrip to check it out. Colonel Rosco was a tall man, wore leather pants and jacket, and of course, a leather cap that buttoned under his chin. His plane looked huge to me with a shiny aluminum body and wicker seats inside. I don't recall what it cost for a ride, but the plane was full of passengers. We roared down the field and I remember the engines making a lot of noise. Mother and I both really enjoyed our ride.

In the early 1940s, Canfield Airport was located on West Donald Street south of where the Waterloo Municipal Airport now stands. The airport had a grass landing strip and one large airplane hangar. After WWII, it was converted to a lumberyard.

During this time, the Civil Air Patrol was headquartered there and a friend of mine asked if I would like to join. It sounded like a lot of fun, so my friend picked me up a form to be filled out and signed by a parent. My mom looked over the form and asked to know more about the Civil Air Patrol. I told her it was like the Boy Scouts except we would learn about airplanes instead of camping. Mother was interested in airplanes so she was willing to sign the form giving her permission.

The first Saturday I went to the Civil Air Patrol Headquarters, I reported to a pilot and gave him the completed consent form. He greeted me with a "Welcome aboard, son!" so I guessed I was now a member of the Civil Air Patrol Cadets.

The Patrol had two single-engine planes made especially for the U.S. Army by the Piper Cub Company. They were called spotter planes and were used to spot locations of enemy armies. Their only defense was large flaps in the wings that could be lowered, causing the plane to almost drop in midair. If an enemy fighter plane tried to shoot them down, the pilot would drop the flaps, the airplane would free fall, and hopefully, the machine guns would miss the plane. Pilot life expectancy was very short over enemy territory.

In the airplane hangar was a meeting room and a small office. On the walls in the meeting room were photographs of German and Japanese bombers and fighter planes so pilots entering the military would be able to identify enemy aircraft. Silhouettes of Japanese battleships, cruisers, and aircraft carriers also hung there for men entering the Navy and Marine Air Force. Pilots needed to be able to recognize silhouettes of Japanese ships so when making torpedo runs, they knew which ships were Japanese Navy and which were U.S. Navy.

I wanted to become a gunner on a Navy torpedo bomber, so I really paid attention to the pilot who taught our class. I learned the names of all the Japanese battleships, cruisers, and aircraft carriers and could identify all the Japanese ships by their silhouette.

The pilot who took my application must have taken a liking to me. I always called him "sir" when speaking to him. Whenever he would practice flying and dropping wing flaps, he always took me with him. Saturdays were the day he flew since he had another job during the week. After a complete check of the plane, away we would go! When in the air, my job was to continually be on the lookout for a safe place to land in case the engine stopped. I would also lower the flaps when the pilot told me. It was fun when the plane would almost stop and drop straight down.

When we had dropped enough to suit him, the pilot yelled, "Pull them in, Tom."

The pilot was training as a spotter pilot in the Army Air Force and I always wondered if he lived through his tour of duty during WWII.

One weekend the pilot asked me if I would be sure to come to the airport the next Saturday because he had been assigned special duty. The Army was training the draftees from Black Hawk County by having war games in the woods along the Cedar River in Josh Higgins Park. The park was named after a famous radio announcer in the area who was liked by everyone, but is now known as George Wyth State Park. We were divided into the Red Army and the Blue Army and loaded the spotter plane with boxes filled with sacks of flour to be used as bombs. As part of the Blue Army, my job was to throw out the sacks of flour as we dived just above the trees over the Red Army. If any soldier got flour on him, he was considered dead. We attacked the Reds over and over until we ran out of sacks of flour. From the air, we could see both armies on the ground and would radio the positions of the Red Army to our Blue Army. I guess it was a little dangerous on my part, because I was flying with the door of the plane open and throwing out the sacks of flour when in a dive. I think we almost whipped the Red Army, because I could see sacks of flour bursting open and hitting the soldiers.

The pilot would yell, "Good job, Tom" as we dived down just above the treetops. We both had a good time bombing the Red Army!

My Uncle Harry was one of the soldiers in the Blue Army. When he learned I was in the airplane staffing the Red Army and dropping flour sacks on them, he said, "Tom, I could see someone throwing sacks of flour from the plane, but I never dreamed it was you!"

Before heading back to the airport, we circled around the Blue Army. They all yelled and raised their guns in the air to celebrate our win over the Red Army. Then, all of a sudden, the motor on the Piper Cub stopped! I could hardly believe my eyes when I saw the propeller stop turning. In case you're wondering … no, we didn't run out of gasoline. It was engine trouble.

The pilot yelled, "We're going down, Tom!"

Remembering my duty when in the air, I yelled back to the pilot, "Look to your left, sir. There is a flat field on the left."

"I see it, Tom. We can glide that far and land in the field," replied the pilot.

Down we went. Wow! It was a field of watermelons, and as we touched ground, I could hear the wheels of the airplane hitting the melons. *Thump, thump, thump.* The pilot was able to keep the plane under control and we made it down safely. If it wasn't for the watermelon field close by, we would have crashed into the trees in Josh Higgins Park.

The pilot said, "Tom, you saved our lives by doing a good job spotting landing sites."

"Sir, you did a great job landing in that watermelon field. Wow, did we ever bust open a lot of watermelons!" I said.

We both had a good laugh, but of course, it was no laughing matter.

Our emergency landing was news and got into the *Waterloo Daily Courier*, a local newspaper, with photographs. Unfortunately, someone showed Mother the article and that was the end of my Civil Air Patrol tour of duty!

About two months later, all the young men of both the Red and Blue Armies, including my Uncle Harry, marched down West Fourth Street in Waterloo and loaded up on a waiting train. The soldiers were heading to an army base for further military training. It seemed that all of Black Hawk County was there shouting and waving flags.

Uncle Harry lived through WWII and the Korean War. Where would you ever find a greater hero than that? As a kid growing up, he was certainly my hero. The sad thing is I didn't see Uncle Harry again for over fifteen years after he marched down West Fourth Street and boarded the train.

CHAPTER 15

Spats

I had just sold my Schwinn bicycle for fifty dollars. I know that was a lot of money during WWII, but my bike was really, really special. It had twin-chrome front headlights, a large tail light, a horn on the front that could be honked by pushing a button on the handle bars, a large chrome luggage rack, and even a speedometer attached to the handle bars; but the most important features were the wheel covers I made to cover the upper half of both rear wheels. I called them "spats." They were really something to see! I designed and made them myself and thought they were probably the only bicycle spats in the world. The idea to call them spats came from watching my Uncle Harry who, in my opinion, was the most handsome man in Black Hawk County! Whenever he would wear his suit out on a date, he always wore spats on top of his dress shoes.

To make the spats, I first removed the luggage rack and the rear wheel. I then made two patterns out of cardboard, transferred the patterns to a piece of sheet metal, and cut them out. Next, I drilled holes in the rear fender and attached the spats with small bolts. Wow! They looked great!

I rode my bike to Red's Body Shop, an automobile repair business, on West Fifth Street to see what it would cost to have them professionally painted. I looked up the owner, explained what I wanted done, and asked how much it would cost. He inspected my work and then looked up and yelled, "Hey, Rod. Come and see what this kid attached to his bike! He calls them spats and wants to know our lowest price to get them painted."

"How much money have you got, kid?" he asked.

"I have a job, sir, delivering newspapers for the *Waterloo Daily Courier*," I replied, "but I only have five dollars."

"Let's take a look at your design."

I showed him what I had drawn on one of the cardboard patterns. "I thought a lightning bolt would look neat."

Rod looked at the owner, winked at him, and said, "What's your name, kid?"

"Tom."

Then Rod said, "Leave your bike and we will paint your spats for five dollars. Come back in a week and I will have them finished."

My spats were being painted by a professional painter and I was all smiles!

When I returned to pick up my bike, the spats were all painted, and they were a knockout!

"How do you like them, Tom?" questioned Rod.

"Oh, they look wonderful! Thank you, Mr. Rod."

He laughed and said he thought they looked nice too.

My bicycle became the talk of the neighborhood and made me think that maybe I could go into business manufacturing spats for bicycles. I thought about all the red-hot designs that could be painted on spats, but at fourteen years old, I had automobile on my mind.

After the spats were installed, my bike was noticed by a twelve-year-old boy who wanted to own it really bad and had his father try to buy it from me. His dad approached me and asked how much I wanted for my bike.

"Sir, my bike is very special with the spats covering the rear wheels and all the nice chrome accessories on it. Fifty bucks or no sale," I told him.

"Egad," he replied. "You drive a hard bargain, kid!"

I now had fifty dollars burning a hole in my pocket and wanted to buy a car with the money.

CHAPTER 16

Geeks

The National Dairy Cattle Congress was located just south of our acreage on Ansborough Avenue. It was held in the fall and the hundreds of cars going to the fair on our gravel road made the house look like it had snowed, the dust was so thick. It didn't bother me any, but Mom hated all that dust, because it penetrated into the house.

In the 1930s and '40s, my Grandfather Shepherd had a tented restaurant on the main strip down the center of the Cattle Congress. He would start frying chickens in the morning and pile them up against the glassed-in counter across the front of the tent, so everyone that walked past could see them. Before noon, the line started to form and became longer and longer. It seemed to me that most everyone had to have Grandpa

Shepherd's chicken! Later, he sold the chicken restaurant and moved to Des Moines, Iowa.

Too Tall and I always had a terrific time at Cattle Congress. The carnival was great, and the rides were a lot of fun too. Mother would give me two dollars to spend and I usually spent it all on the rides. The money was supposed to be for an admission ticket and lunch, but we thought that would be dumb. Too Tall and I never bought tickets. There were plenty of places to just walk in.

Every year we hunted up the Alstadt and Langlas Bakery booth and got in line for a free, miniature loaf of bread given away as advertising. Too Tall and I would get in line over and over again until we were noticed and stopped, but we usually had three or four loaves by then. When we became hungry, we would step into a hotdog joint, try to find a seat, and make bread and ketchup sandwiches. The owners usually noticed we were using their ketchup and kicked us out.

Next door to the Cattle Congress grounds was the Electric Park Ballroom. Big Band dances were held every Saturday night. All the popular bands, like Tommy Dorsey and Glen Miller, had a gig at the Electric Park Ballroom. Some of the hit songs at the time were "Beer Barrel Polka," "Lovely to Look At," "The Music Goes Round and Around," and "I Got Plenty of Nuttin.'" After I bought my

Model A, Too Tall and I would always go dancing on Saturday night.

We especially had a great time when the Waves would be on weekend leave from their barracks at the Teacher's College in Cedar Falls. They all wore white dress uniforms, and that was a special sight to see! Too Tall and I were younger and couldn't dance very well, but they didn't mind. All the young men were away serving their country, and we were available.

Too Tall and I learned a dance called The Shag. We liked the dance because it didn't matter what kind of music was played, the shag would work.

The Waves were required to return to their barracks by 11:00 PM, so we would ask a few of the girls if they would like a ride back to Cedar Falls. They always said yes, and, after crowding in, one girl would have to sit on Too Tall's lap. The next day, all Too Tall could talk about was his ride to Cedar Falls with a good looking Wave on his lap!

One Saturday night, we were at the dance and heard a lot of cursing and swearing going on at the bar. I walked over to see what was happening and could hardly believe my eyes. There was Clarence Fike! When I first started attending Edison School, I had to walk past the Fike's house, and Clarence would get one of his younger brothers to stop me and start a fight with him. It usually came out even-steven, so they finally left me alone.

Recently, Clarence had been wounded in a naval battle in the South Pacific, and his right arm was bandaged up and in a sling. He was arguing with a Marine home on leave, and it was a real shouting match. Clarence called the Marine a lot of bad names, and out the door they went. The cut off to the Cedar River was behind the Electric Park, and there was a long downhill grade to get to the river. Clarence and the Marine were both drunk and started fighting. They were punching each other pretty good, got too close to the drop off to the river, and down they went! When they landed, the fight was over. The bartender called the police, and the police hauled them both to jail. I think Clarence needed an ambulance, but he was a really tough guy. He had several brothers and all they did was fight.

After Clarence was discharged from the Navy, he became a mail carrier for the Waterloo Post Office.

The Electric Park Ballroom was open all summer and had a few small carnival rides. Too Tall's and my favorite was a huge barrel that turned slowly, around and around. If you fell down, you continued to go around, and it was difficult to get back on your feet.

Another attraction was the Geek Show. I know it would not be allowed today. The Geeks had a wagon with steel bars all around it, similar to a jail cell. They were really bad alcoholics, and this is how they made their living. After collecting as much money from the crowd as they could, the show would begin. A Geek would get inside the wagon and an assistant would throw in a live chicken. The Geek would catch it, pull off its head with his teeth, and drink the blood as it spewed out. Too Tall and I would laugh as he drank the chicken's blood. We both had to cut chicken's heads off for our mothers when they wanted to have fried chicken for dinner. Needless to say, the Geek Show was short-lived!

Many now-married couples first met at the Electric Park Ballroom, and to this day, it is still going strong!

CHAPTER 17

Yellow-Spoke Wheels

One day Too Tall said to me, "Tom, you have been talking about buying a car and I know a lady who wants to sell her Model A Ford."

"I sure would like to see it!" I said to Too Tall. "Can we go take a look?"

We walked about two miles to the woman's house on Hawthorne Avenue and knocked on the door. When she answered, I asked if she had a car for sale. She explained that the car was for sale because her husband had passed away and she did not know how to drive. We went outside to the garage in back of the house and she handed me the key to unlock the door. I unlocked the door and tried to open it, but the door was stuck. Too Tall helped me give it a shove and light rushed in as we slid it to one side.

What a wonderful sight! I thought the moment could have been put to music: "Oh, what a beautiful mornin', Oh, what a beautiful day!"

Too Tall said, "You OK, Tom?"

I couldn't believe it! There right before me was a black 1929 Model A Ford Fordor with bright yellow-spoke wheels sitting on concrete blocks. It almost took my breath away.

Too Tall said it again, "You OK, Tom?"

I opened the driver's side door and looked inside. The car was in almost showroom condition. The seats were perfect and everything, including the manifold heater on the floor of the passenger's side, was in tip-top shape. As I walked around the car, I could find no dents or scratches. World War II had made rubber tires as scarce as hen's teeth, but my dream car had four almost brand-new tires and the spare had never been used! Too Tall looked at me and smiled the biggest smile his face could make.

"Ma'am, I have fifty dollars cash," I said.

"Say no more, son," the woman replied. "If you want the car, fifty dollars will do."

Too Tall almost choked. He couldn't believe I had made such a keen deal. I gave the woman the money and told her I would be back as soon as I could to get my car. I wanted to say, "I will be back to get my dream come true!"

Too Tall and I walked home, gathered up what I thought we would need to get the Model A started and headed back to get the car. As soon as we arrived, I checked the oil and put in a gallon of gas we had drained out of Too Tall's dad's car. We pumped air in the tires, jacked up each wheel, and removed the concrete blocks. I slid the transmission into neutral, set the choke levers, and went around to the front of the car. Then I stuck in the crank and gave it a powerful quarter of a turn. Holy Cow! Was I excited! I did know enough not to turn the crank completely around, because it could backfire and break my arm.

Out of the tailpipe came a loud explosive noise. *Bang! Bang! Pop! Pop!* And then the engine began running as smoothly as a railroad pocket watch. I hurried to get in the driver's seat, pushed in the clutch pedal, and shifted into first gear. Giving her a little gas, I slowly let out the clutch and out of the garage I went! Too Tall closed and locked the garage door and got in the car. We waved to the nice old woman who had sold me my dream come true, and down Hawthorne Avenue we sailed.

How did a fourteen-year-old know how to drive a car? My older brother had a 1936 Ford and he would let me drive whenever we went someplace together.

"Holy Smoke," Too Tall said. "Let's see how fast she will go!"

"I better not until I get used to driving her," I wisely replied.

I dropped Too Tall at his house, and as I drove off, Too Tall yelled, clapped his hands, and jumped up and down in approval of what we had done.

My generation fell in love with the automobile. Motoring around could bring wonderful adventures, especially for a fourteen-year-old boy behind the wheel of a Model A Fordor with bright yellow-spoke wheels. I bet Henry Ford was smiling, maybe laughing, and maybe a little faint, if he knew how my imagination was fired up!

I drove home and parked my prize out back by the chicken coop. Mother, of course, noticed my Model A when she came home from work.

Her first question was, "Whose car is parked out back?"

I told her I had sold my bicycle for fifty dollars and used the money to buy the car.

"Isn't it a beauty?" I said.

" You're only fourteen years old and don't have a driver's license. What am I going to do with you?"

She thought a minute and then added, "I guess it's all right that you bought the car, but you are only allowed to drive it in a circle out back until you can get a driver's license."

Whew! Getting that settled was easier than I thought! I really believed I would have more trouble than that from Mom.

I circled around the backyard two times and that was enough for me. Out on the street I went!

At that time, gas was rationed because of the war, and Mom knew I could only get three gallons a week. I guess she thought I couldn't get into too much trouble on only three gallons of gas. She definitely miscalculated!

I knew only three gallons of gas would cut my adventures short, but I quickly learned a Model A Ford could run on more than just gasoline. I would pour in my three gallons of gas, add a small can of Wynn's Friction Proofing Oil, and then fill the rest of the tank with fuel oil. One quarter of a turn and a bang and that gem of a four-cylinder engine would be running just fine. I also had a good friend who worked at a DX gas station. If he was working alone, we would use a stamp to put in seven gallons of gasoline and three gallons of fuel oil. Gas rationing didn't stop me from driving my 1929 Model A Fordor to wherever my next adventure awaited!

CHAPTER 18

Christmas Reflections

Part 1

Christmas in 1933 was at the height of the Great Depression. My mother would buy several hams from work at a discount. Then we loaded up the hams, jars of vegetables, candy canes for the children, and if it looked like we would have enough potatoes to last through the winter, we also packed a few paper sacks of potatoes to deliver to friends who had lost their jobs or were destitute. Our first stop was on Fowler Street where we lived before moving across town to our acreage.

We knocked and when Mable answered the door and saw the food, she said, "Oh, Emma!" and started to cry.

We went in the house and visited a short time when Mom said, "We have to go now, Mable. Have a good Christmas!"

"We will now, Emma!" and she started crying again. I didn't quite understand what was going on, but Mom sure made them happy.

Part 2

Our next stop was across the Cedar River in the Riverview Addition. The man of the house answered the door and when he saw the ham, he said, "Gosh, Emma, I guess we will have a good Christmas after all! Thank you so much."

Mom said, "How are you doing, Earl? Where is your garage?"

"I sold the garage a couple of months ago. We didn't need it since I had to sell my car to survive, and now we will start selling some of the furniture. We have to have food. The County Welfare Board got me a job shoveling off a whole train car of coal, but I was only paid eight dollars. I miss my car, but I rode my bicycle to the Black Hawk County sheds to unload the coal. We are surviving and now that ham will make our Christmas! Thank you, Emma."

Part 3

I remember one family who lived on Fowler Street whose water and electricity had been shut off. They had to walk the railroad tracks just to get a little coal to heat the house. I know because I needed to go the bathroom and Mother whispered, "No. There is no water to flush the stool." The family was so very thankful for the food, and the Mrs. even cried!

Mom drove us around town to the rest of her friends to help them have a good Christmas. I know we always had a happy Christmas. Mom saw to that!

Part 4

We drove to Grandma Friedrichs' house in Elgin, Iowa for Christmas. Our car was an Indian Tan, four-door Chevrolet. It was a beauty!

I believe Uncle Hans and my first cousin, Marvel, were there, also. We always had plenty of good German food at Grandma's house. My Christmas present was a small army of little lead soldiers from Santa Claus.

Helene Koopman Friedrichs Family;
Front Row: Emma, Adolph, Harry, Helene, Hans;
Back Row: William, Adolph, Minnie

Part 5

It was 1953 and Christmas was coming! I was a young fireman at the headquarters station in downtown Waterloo. We took up a collection for needy families and the local undertaker always stopped and gave us a donation also. We called him "Digger," and he would do anything for the firemen! He was given a silver badge from the International Association of Fire Fighters, and it was the only one ever given to a civilian. We would say, "Let's see your badge, Digger!" If he didn't have it on him, he had to buy ice cream for the crew. At the time, there were fourteen men stationed at headquarters.

Part 6

Across the street from the fire station was a Goodyear Tire Store that sold toys during the Christmas season. The manager knew we were coming and agreed to sell us the toys at bargain prices. After dark, both black and white children would start to show up at the station. None had the luxury of receiving a Christmas present that year, but they all knew the firemen would be there for them. One at a time, we would take them across the street to choose a toy since we were still going to fires if any calls came in. Some of the boys were only five years old and their families could not afford any gifts for them. When my turn came, I took a little black boy and asked his name. "T.V. Williams, and please, sir, could you also buy a toy for my little sister?" he replied.

"Sure. Pick one out for her too," I said.

I would bet those children still remember the firemen at Station One. In later years, T.V. Williams would visit the fire station and always asked to see Fireman Tom!

Part 7

We also had homeless men show up at the station on Christmas Eve. We would feed them, wash their clothes, cut their hair, and allow them to take a shower. One fellow came every year and had so much dirt caked on his neck that we used a straight razor to get it off.

Part 8

My wife, Eunice, and I now go to estate sales during the year and buy blankets for needy and homeless people. This year we also went to a swap meet and purchased stocking hats and gloves, since at night the temperature gets down to forty-five degrees. You can't let yourself think about it or you might shed a few tears.

CHAPTER 19

Model A

One splendid Iowa summer's day, I was sitting on the front porch with my collie dog, Pat, at my feet. The weather was warm, but pleasant in the shade. When we were alone, I would talk to Pat and it seemed as though he understood what I said to him. My Model A was parked in the driveway and I told Pat I was thinking of tearing down the engine. I wanted to see what the inside of an engine looked like. Pat jumped to his feet and looked up at me. I believe he was thinking, *Are you crazy?*

"Let's go, Pat!" I said excitedly to my companion.

He ran to the car and I opened the door so he could jump in. We drove downtown to J and R Auto Parts Store. I told the clerk what I wanted to do and that as long as I had the engine torn apart, I might as well put in new rings.

"I have ten bucks, sir," I said. "Will that cover the cost?"

He penciled down some figures and said, "Ten bucks will cover what you need. By golly, you sure are a spunky kid. What's your name?"

"Tom," I replied.

He started to give me some good advice about tearing down my engine and I said, "Let me go out to the car and get my notebook. I want to write everything down that is important."

I purchased three rings for each cylinder. The lower ring was an oil regulating ring and the upper two rings were compression rings. I also bought a gasket kit, valve cover kit, four spark plugs and five quarts of oil. The clerk set the proper gap on the spark plugs and said to call if I had any trouble.

I drove home and parked in the front yard under the shade of a beautiful maple tree. I raised the hood and looked at the engine. The engine was too hot to get started right away, so I unhooked the hood clamps, removed the hood, and leaned it against the tree. Pat sauntered over, smelled around the hood, and then stretched out on the grass. He was ready to wait until the "Shade Tree Mechanic" was finished with the engine overhaul.

Mom returned from work and, looking at the situation, shook her head and went in the house. I got off easy again!

The next morning, I started dismantling the engine.

"Ashes to ashes, dust to dust. If it wasn't for Fords, our tools would rust!"

I removed the spark plugs, took off the header, and pulled out the battery. In a small notebook, I wrote the date and made notes so I would know where the parts came from and how to reassemble them correctly. I certainly wish I had kept that notebook. It would be very interesting to read today!

Next, I jacked up the car and, to be safe, placed some concrete blocks underneath in case the jack fell over. The oil pan was removed and I tried to catch it all, but was soon covered with greasy oil. After gathering all the rags I could find in the house and barn, I removed the connecting rods and piston assembly from the cylinder block. The engine was new enough that it did not have a ridge worn at the top of the block, which made removal of the pistons easier. I used a wooden hammer handle to tap them out. Since the firing order was 1-3-4-2, I marked a number on each connecting rod cap with a steel punch so I could reinstall the caps on the proper rod.

Afterward, I unattached the gaskets, stripped off the old sealing compound, and cleaned the carbon from the cylinder block and head. No damage was found on the cylinder block, studs, water pump, or pulley. Even though it was difficult without a ring remover, I was able to extract the piston rings. I unfastened the piston lock screws and pushed the piston pin out. Carbon was scraped from the ring grooves in the pistons and the oil holes in the oil ring were cleaned. The pistons had no cracks, scores, or damage of any kind, and the piston ring grooves showed no wear. I had trouble fitting the new piston rings on the cylinder, but I was determined to get them on. I pressed the pistons halfway down into the cylinder bore so the ring would be square with the cylinder wall. Using a feeler gage, I measured the gap to be an acceptable .008. The connecting rods were not bent or twisted, and the connecting rod insert bearings, caps, and lock nuts were all satisfactory. No valves were eroded, burned, warped, or pitted. I cleaned all parts and passages with cleaning solvent. Wow! Did I make a mess on the lawn!

Reinstalling the oil pan was difficult to do by myself and Too Tall had gone to Boy Scout Camp the week I was working on my car. I had to hold a gasket and oil intake float in place and install four lock nut washers and cap screws by myself.

Next, the crankcase needed to be filled with grease. Ever hear of a grease monkey? That was me! I was covered with grease and oil after installing the oil pan.

I checked for foreign material in the cylinders, placed the cylinder head gasket on the block, and tightened the cylinder head bolts by starting with a centrally located bolt and working both ways.

The new spark plugs were installed and the spark plug wires connected. I made sure the radiator and engine drain cocks were closed, reinstalled everything written down in my notebook, filled the radiator with water and screwed the hood back on. Pat sensed I was close to being finished and jumped up to watch.

I bet by now you are wondering how a fourteen-year-old boy could install new rings in his Model A Fordor engine. Most kids today could not tear apart a bicycle, let alone an automobile engine, but the Model A had a very simple and uncomplicated engine.

I had one more thing I wanted to do. A wire was hooked to the choke lever, run down near the crank and looped on the end so I could choke the engine when I turned the crank.

Pat was watching and wagged his tail. I inserted the crank, pulled the choke wire a little, gave the crank a quarter turn and the engine started! I thought I was the best Shade Tree Mechanic in town!

My Model A Ford was now running perfectly. What a wonderful sound the engine made with the new rings I had installed! Too Tall showed up and couldn't believe how easily the engine started after the work I had done.

One lesson I learned was that it is a lot more difficult to put an engine back together than it is to tear it down, but I was able to get the job done.

After I got the engine running, I cleaned the car inside and out. Holy Cow! Was I proud of my achievement! I owned a 1929 Model A Fordor with new rings and spark plugs, all paid for, and was now ready to see how fast she would go!

In a Model A, traveling at forty-two miles an hour was really tearing down the road! The first time I drove that fast, Too Tall and Pat were with me and I think we all were a little scared.

Owning a Model A gave me considerable freedom and provided for countless adventures. It presented many learning experiences, hard knocks of the very best kind, and the opportunity to learn considerable mechanical knowledge. For a fourteen-year-old boy, it was a wonderful life!

CHAPTER 20

Buzz Coil

Too Tall and I went to visit Jim Van Nice, a friend of ours. His dad said to me, "Tom would you like to have some fun with your Model A?"

I said, "Sure. What can I do?"

"You will have to go to an auto salvage yard and purchase a Model T Ford buzz coil. Jim told me you have already put new rings in the engine, so I bet you will have no trouble doing what I have in mind. With the buzz coil, you can make the car put out a slight electrical shock to anyone who touches the body and is grounded, especially if the ground is wet. It is harmless, though, and won't hurt anyone."

"Gosh, Mr. Van Nice, that would be fun! Let me get my notebook and write everything down."

He listed the parts I needed and wrote instructions on how to install it. Then Too Tall and I headed for the nearest auto salvage yard. I needed a buzz coil, some wire, a piece of strap metal, and a toggle switch. While we looked around, I found an absolutely beautiful gearshift knob for fifty cents. It was made of glass with shimmering colors inside and fit on the shifter and to my hand perfectly. The extra weight of the glass knob made it easier and faster to shift into the forward gears.

I was able to purchase a buzz coil for a dollar. It was made of wood and inside were four outlets to the timer, four outlets to the spark plugs, and one outlet to the magneto. I mounted the buzz coil on the firewall of the car with metal plumbing strap. The four outside connections went to the battery, the timer, the engine block, and one for a ground. I hooked up a power switch on the dash to activate the buzz coil from the battery. At the ground connection, I attached the metal strap that dragged under the car so the buzz coil was always grounded. Anyone who touched the car with the power switch on would receive a small electrical shock. GOSH! MAYBE THIS WAS THE FIRST THEFT DETERRENT SYSTEM FOR AN AUTOMOBILE!

One day, I flipped the switch as my collie dog, Pat, smelled around the right rear wheel and lifted his leg. The buzz coil worked and Pat never lifted his leg on my Model A again!

I had another thought. Too Tall lived a short distance down the street in a salvaged railroad passenger car. It was very long and had lots of windows. At the time, I thought it was the neatest house in town.

Too Tall's swimming suit was in my car so I got it wet, wrung it out, and placed it on the passenger side door ledge. The horn blared *oogah, oogah* and out came Too Tall.

I threw the switch and yelled, "Get your swimming suit."

He grabbed the suit and was surprised with a shock. Then I explained what was going on and we had a good laugh. We talked about all the possibilities and things we could do with my buzz coil-charged Model A.

We headed for downtown Waterloo, but stopped about five blocks down the street at Edison School playground. "Hi, kids!" I said. "Want to have some fun? Just join hands and the first person in line, touch my car."

About ten of them joined hands and I flipped the toggle switch. The charge tingled through all of them, but the boy on the end really got a jolt! That scared me and I got out and ran to him. To my relief, he was unhurt and I never did that again!

We continued downtown and parked behind a sleek, four-door, black Buick. I pulled up close enough to touch the chrome bumper. Soon the owner appeared and I flipped the switch. We could see he was getting a small shock when he touched the door handle. He jerked his hand away and looked quite puzzled. After touching the door again and getting another shock, he opened the door this time and drove off in that dandy Buick! He could have caught on and caused me a lot of trouble, so I never tried to shock an adult again.

When you owned a car, it was quite easy to attract girls. Sometimes the girls would walk over, and while visiting with us, lean on the car. I flipped the toggle switch and they would get an electrical tingle. The girls would sometimes yell, but it didn't really hurt. The buzz coil worked like a cat's meow. It was really fun to play with.

Occasionally, I would ask the girls if they would like to go to Overland's Ice Cream Parlor and get a double dipper. Back then, it only cost a nickel! We always made sure it was dark by the time we finished, because behind Overland's was a really, really steep hill down to the railroad tracks toward the John Deere tractor factory. I would turn off the lights, shift into first gear, and down the hill we went! The girls were scared to death and would scream, but I could get the car stopped just before hitting the railroad tracks. Going down that sharp grade in the dark and hearing the girls scream was more fun than a roller coaster!

CHAPTER 21

Devil's Backbone

One day I said to Too Tall, "Let's go to Backbone State Park next Sunday and have a picnic."

Backbone State Park is located about forty miles from Waterloo near the town of Dundee. The State of Iowa Fish Hatchery stocked several trout streams that run through the park and then join the scenic Maquoketa River. The several hundred acres of woods are filled with hickory, maple, and oak trees. The park contains a small lake and the hills are limestone rock. One especially high limestone formation is called The Devil's Backbone.

"Jiminy Cricket, that would be fun!" said Too Tall.

"You know, Too Tall, if we take a couple of girls along, we would get to help them up the Devil's Backbone."

"Tom, how come you know so much?" Too Tall asked.

"Well, I'm a year older than you. I'm fourteen, remember?"

Too Tall invited a girl who lived near Edison School and I invited Sally Sue. Her parents owned the ice cream parlor near the Electric Park Ballroom. I believe she liked me, because whenever I went there she made me my favorite malted milk—chocolate marshmallow with a couple of cherries on top—at no charge!

Both girls agreed to go and even packed us a lunch. I made sure the car was gassed up and clean inside and out.

Pat and I picked everyone up early Sunday morning. The girls knew lots of songs and, as we drove, had a wonderful time singing with Too Tall and me joining in. Pat had a great time, too, with all the petting and extra attention from the girls.

A few of the songs we enjoyed singing along the way were:

Fly's in the buttermilk, Shoo, fly, shoo,
Fly's in the buttermilk, Shoo, fly, shoo,

Fly's in the buttermilk, Shoo, fly, shoo,
Skip to my Lou, my darlin'

A bushel an' a peck and a hug around the neck
Hug around the neck and a barrel an' a heap.
Barrel an' a heap an' I'm talking in my sleep.
About you, about me? Yes, about you.
My heart is leapin', havin' trouble sleepin'
'Cause I love you a barrel an' a heap.
You bet your purdy neck I do.

Roll out the barrel. We'll have a barrel of fun.
Roll out the barrel. We've got the blues on the run.

Show me the way to go home.
I'm tired and I want to go to bed.
I had a little drink about an hour ago
And it went right to my head.
Where ever I may roam
On land or sea or foam,
You will always hear me singing this song.
Show me the way to go home.

As we drove along the highway, we saw several Burma Shave signs. They were always fun to read. A few of our favorites we saw beside the road were:

*Don't stick your arm out. The window's too far.
It might go home in another car.*

*Passing school zone. Take it slow. Let our little
shavers grow.*

*Folks wouldn't feel in so much danger if we still
had the old Lone Ranger.*

*My wardrobe now, one thing it lacks. Bloomers
made from flour sacks.*

The girls screamed and laughed when they
read that Burma Shave sign!

Too Tall and I also practiced our Pig Latin,
but were not sure if the girls understood. "Want
to hear a couple of Ford jokes, Too Tall?" I said.

"Ouyay etbay, Omtay!" replied Too Tall. (You
bet, Tom!)

"Uybay a ordFay. Uybay hetay estbay. Riveday
a ilemay. Alkway hetay estray." (Buy a Ford. Buy
the best. Drive a mile. Walk the rest.)

"I ouldcay evernay eepkay a ordFay nderuay
emay. I asway lwaysay nderuay hetay ordFay." (I
could never keep a Ford under me. I was always
under the Ford.)

We arrived at the park safely and drove
through two trout streams that crossed the road.
We promptly found a pleasant spot near a fire
pit to eat our picnic lunch and I parked the car

nearby. "Let's go climb up the Devil's Backbone," I said excitedly.

Everybody yelled, "Yea! Let's go!"

Pat joined in the excitement, because he knew that whatever we were going to do, he would be a part of it too. We followed the signs and found the way. It was quite steep and a long walk, so we helped the girls to the top. It was great fun!

Afterward we walked back down to the car and retrieved our lunch. We built a fire, roasted hot dogs, and ate all the good food the girls had brought with them. Pat loved the girls, because they both fed him scraps of food!

After lunch, we all got into the car and drove to the lake. It was a beautiful drive, seeing all the hills and trees, and it was warm enough to go swimming. We found the beach house and put on our swimming suits and Too Tall reminded me how I had once shocked him when he grabbed his suit off the car door. We laughed about it again!

Too Tall and I ran for the water and jumped in. We swam out into the lake and I'll swear on a stack of Bibles that two girls were out in the lake wearing only men's swim suits! They were about sixteen and very mature. I swam near one of the girls and talked with her a bit. They had never been off the farm in their entire lives! They told me all they did was work, work, work and never got away from it all until today.

I told Too Tall, "I bet their dad kept them on the farm almost like slaves, because he had no help to hire."

Most able-bodied men were drafted into the army. He may have had to use the girls like hired hands or possibly lose the farm.

Then Too Tall and I swam back to shore and stretched out on our blankets in the sun. Pat was also having a great time running around and splashing in the lake.

Later, we walked around the park and enjoyed the scenery. A couple of fellows were trout fishing in the stream near us, and we watched them for a while.

Before long, we needed to be heading back to Waterloo. When I announced it was time to go home, Too Tall and the girls all yelled, "Oh, no!" at the same time.

Pat could sense something was up and started to bark. It was all great fun! Too Tall winked at me. He had a great time just like I told him he would.

CHAPTER 22

Sucker Punch

I t was spring, the sun was finally shining, and the ground was warming. Everything growing seemed to be moving upward.

About two hundred feet north of our house, I heard a banging and pounding noise, so I jumped into my Model A Ford and drove down the street to pick up my good buddy, Too Tall. We then drove over to see what it was all about. A large machine was digging a hole in the ground and piling the dirt up into a huge mound. A man stood near watching, and I asked him if he knew what the hole in the ground was for.

"We are digging a basement and I'm going to build a house here as soon as we get the block laid. My name is Mr. Van Nice. Where do you boys live?" he asked.

"We live just down the street. Mine is the white house with the front porch, and my friend, Too Tall, lives in the converted railroad car. My name is Tom and my friend's name is Richie, but we call him Too Tall."

"Well, I like that name," Mr. Van Nice laughed. "I've got a son around here someplace and he is really big for his age. I should have named him Too Tall, but his name is Jim. You own that Model A, son?"

"Yes, sir," I replied.

"You look awfully young to own a car. How old are you?"

"I'm fourteen years old, but will be fifteen on October 6 and I can get my driver's license in Cedar Falls on that day."

"Want to hear a wild story?" I added. "Last night I was across town visiting a girl friend of mine. She is in my confirmation class at First Lutheran Church. It was late, around one in the morning, and I was heading down Falls Avenue towards home. I was alone and there was no traffic so I had the gas pedal pushed to the floor. My car's top speed is forty-five, so I guess I was cruising along at about forty. All of a sudden I heard a siren. It was a police officer wanting me to pull over and stop. The officer got out of his police car and approached my Model A."

He looked inside and said, "Say, kid, did you know you were speeding? Let me see your driver's license."

"Sorry, sir," I answered. "I don't have a driver's license. They won't allow me to have one."

"Who is 'they'?" he asked.

"The State of Iowa. You must be fifteen to get a license to drive a car."

"Who does this car belong to?"

"It is mine, and I paid fifty dollars for it. The State of Iowa let me buy a Model A, but I guess they don't want me to drive it," I said.

"What's your name, kid?"

"Tom Shepherd," I told the officer.

"By golly, I knew your dad! You're Ben Shepherd's kid. Did you know he was a policeman? He was a cop for about two years and then quit and went to work for the Iowa Public Service Company. Your dad was a good police officer. Everyone on the force liked him."

"I knew my dad was a lineman for the Iowa Public Service Company," I said. "When I was eleven, he was working during a storm when a transformer blew up, and he was killed.. I was very young when my parents divorced, so the first time I remember seeing my dad was in his casket, and they were getting ready to put him in the ground."

"I know all about it, Tommy. I'm sorry. Now you slow that Model A down, get your driver's license as soon as you can, and get your butt home."

I stepped out of my car, gave her a turn on the crank, and home I went.

"Hey," Mr. Van Nice said to us, "Here comes my son, Jim." He then turned to Jim and said, "These boys are going to be our neighbors."

He introduced us to his son, as Too Tall and I shook his hand.

"You fellows like boxing?" Mr. Van Nice asked.

"We sure do!" Too Tall said. "Tom and I think Joe Louis, the Brown Bomber, is the greatest. When that German boxer, Max Schmeling, knocked out Joe Lewis, we thought the world would end."

"Do you know how he figured out how to knock out the Brown Bomber? He watched moving pictures of Joe Lewis over and over and noticed that he hesitated for a split second just before he threw a left hook. That's all that German heavyweight needed to know. The first time Joe Lewis threw a left hook, he hesitated, and Schmeling knocked him out."

Their rematch in 1938 didn't last long though. Joe Lewis dropped Max Schmeling in two minutes and four seconds of round one and successfully defended his heavyweight title four times in 1940.

The American People loved Joe Lewis because he said, "We are going to win this war, because God is on our side." And they hated Max Schmeling because he hobnobbed with Adolph Hitler.

Mr. Van Nice's house went up quickly. It was a small story-and-a-half and, as soon as the basement was laid, his two brothers who were carpenters helped him build the rest. The bathroom was outside in the outhouse, and the heating system was a coal-fired furnace.

Mr. Van Nice built a boxing ring in the basement and showed us everything he knew about boxing. We worked out and boxed every day, mostly in the evening hours when Mr. Van Nice could be there to train us. I got so I could handle myself in the ring quite well. Jim Van Nice was a lot larger and a little taller than me, but I could stand up to him and get my licks in. Have you ever heard people say they were hit so hard they saw stars? Well, that's the truth! Once Jim gave me an uppercut and almost knocked me out. I saw stars—lots of stars!

Summer was coming to an end and I had to think about what I could do to protect the radiator in my car from the freezing winter Iowa

129

weather. Antifreeze was not available, and I tried alcohol, but it would boil out.

One fall day I drove over near West Junior High School and stopped at a house near the school. I cannot believe I had the courage, but I was desperate. After ringing the doorbell, a very nice lady answered.

I said, "Ma'am, I am enrolled in West Junior High this coming winter and will have to drain the radiator of my car after I get there. After school, could I please get enough hot water from you to fill the radiator so I can make it home?"

"You sure can," she said and even showed me where a key for the door was hidden so I could get water if she was not at home.

I could hardly believe how nice she was to me!

At night, after I was finished driving for the day, I would drain the radiator and throw a blanket over the engine. Then I had to fill it again in the morning, drive to school, drain it again, refill it with water, and then drive home.

I believe I was the only kid who drove his own car to West Junior High School. One day, a friend of mine told me a senior student named John McCaffery was jealous of me having my own car and driving it to school and planned to beat me up. I told my friend that was dumb, but I would keep a lookout for him. He made a big mistake thinking he could whip me just because he was taller and larger than me. Of course, he didn't know that I had been boxing and working out on a punching bag most of the summer and fall. My friend, Jim Van Nice, overheard McCaffery bragging to some girls he wanted to impress how he was going to beat me up after school.

As soon as classes were out, Jim told me to look out for McCaffery. "I believe he is going to start a fight with you today after school."

The news about the fight spread throughout the school, and it seemed as if half the student body came out to watch. I cut across the tennis courts to the lady's house to get the water for my radiator. McCaffery must have seen me go there before, because he was waiting for me.

Too Tall and Jim were there also, and I told them quickly, "I guess I have to fight that screwball, but you guys stay out of the way unless he trips me and gets me on the ground. Then step in. He is a lot heavier than me, and if he gets me on the ground, he could hurt me bad."

"Don't worry, Tom," Too Tall said. "We'll look out for you."

McCaffery confronted me and was mumbling something about me being a smart-ass owning my own car, and he was going to fix that.

He was not very coordinated. I punched him a couple of times and stepped quickly aside. I

131

didn't hesitate like Joe Lewis when I threw a left hook and hit him in the side of the face. I believe John McCaffery wished he hadn't started a fight with me. Jim and Too Tall cheered me on. I raised my left hand in the air and he looked up at it. I gave him a sucker punch to his nose with my right hand, and he was on the ground, no more fight left in him. It was a lot of excitement, but that was the end of the fight.

"Get in the car, you guys. I'll drive us home," I said to my friends.

Jim Van Nice was smiling from ear to ear. He could hardly wait to get home and tell his dad all about the fight and how I hit that bully with a sucker punch!

CHAPTER 23

Flour City Box Company

In the late 1930s and early 1940s, the economy was changing fast. The Great Depression was ending and World War II was beginning. Just down the street from where I lived was a business called the Flour City Box Company where pop cases were made for Pepsi, Coca Cola, and other soda companies. The government also needed all sizes and shapes of boxes to hold military ammunition. The Flour City Box Company received a large government contract to build boxes for the military and that was the end of making soda pop cases.

The plant was located on a siding track of the Illinois Central Railroad. The ICRR would park trainloads of rough lumber on the siding track nearest the building, and workers would place a ramp from the boxcar right into the factory.

After school was out for the summer in 1940, I walked into the small office attached to the side of the building where a Jewish fellow sat at a desk.

He looked up as I entered and said, "Can I help you?"

"Yes," I replied. "I'm looking for a summer job."

"How old are you?" he questioned.

"I'm fifteen, sir," I told him.

He could tell I was not fifteen, but the company was desperate for help.

"We could really use you," he said. "I will give you a tour of the plant and show you what your job would be. Then if you are still interested, you can start anytime you want. Before we begin the tour, though, I want you to understand that you are not to touch any band saws, table saws, or anything with a saw blade on it. I really mean that. If anyone wants you to run a saw, you come directly to me."

We began the tour and, holy cow, it seemed like a hundred table saws, planers, and band saws were all running at the same time.

As a man with all of his arms, legs, and fingers intact approached the Jewish fellow, he turned to me and said, "This is Mike and he will be your foreman. Gosh, I don't even know your name, son."

"It's Tom, sir. Tom Shepherd."

"Mike will take you around, and when you are finished, come back to the office. You will need to sign some papers."

As the Jewish fellow headed back to his office, Mike turned to me and said, "I want to tell you something before we start. All of our workers are either ex-convicts or are crippled. You and I will be the only workers who are ... well, I don't know what to say."

As we walked to the area where I would be working, Mike continued, "There is absolutely no smoking in the building. Most all of the workers chew tobacco, and they will probably offer you some, but it is up to you if you want to chew. Here is where you will work unloading lumber from the boxcars, and when they are all unloaded, you will haul saw dust."

"Thanks for showing me around, Mike," I said.

I headed back to the office to sign my papers. I said I would take the job and asked if I could start tomorrow.

"Sure! Be here at 7:00 AM."

I returned home and told Mom that I landed a summer job at the Flour City Box Factory.

She said, "That's great, Tom! What will you be doing?"

"I'm not allowed to touch any saws. I will be unloading lumber and hauling saw dust."

I was amazed at how good all the other workers were to me. I guess it didn't make any difference to me what was wrong with them, and they must have sensed that, so they all treated me like I was a long lost son.

I was offered some Red Man chewing tobacco and started chewing and spitting all day just like they did. I actually had a good time with all of the other workers. At break time, they had interesting stories to tell about how they lost an arm or leg. I would listen intently, and I guess they liked that.

After I had worked about a week, the foreman was told to send me to the office.

The young Jewish fellow who hired me said, "The foreman says you are a good worker and everyone seems to like you. I wasn't sure that would happen, but I'm glad you fit in. Tom, I called you in to ask if you know anything about golfing."

I must have looked puzzled, so he explained that he needed a caddy.

"I hope you will enjoy coming to Sunnyside Country Club with me. If you don't know anything about golfing, I will teach you. Mike told me you are a fast learner and I have a tee time at 10:30. Would you like to accompany me as my caddy?"

"Wow, sir. Am I dressed good enough?"

"You're just fine. I've told Mike you will be leaving at 9:30, so just come to the office then."

I returned to the office at the appointed time and the clubs were near the door.

I picked them up and said, "I'm ready."

He winked at the secretary and said, "Let's go, Tom."

We walked out to his Cadillac parked in the driveway, and he opened the trunk.

I put in the clubs and started to get in the back seat, but he said, "Get in the front seat with me, Tom."

We talked all the way to the club. He asked me a lot of questions. Where did I live? Did I have any family old enough to go into the military? I told him my Uncle Harry had been drafted and I thought my brother, Bob, was thinking of enlisting in the Army.

When we arrived at the golf course, my boss changed. It was all golf, because he was a serious and very proficient golfer. I noticed money changing hands. He explained what was expected of me and how to keep his clubs and golf balls clean. I was really happy to be his caddy. It sure beat unloading lumber!

Before teeing off the first hole, he took me aside and said, "Do you see the caddy shack over there? Don't ever go near it. Stay close to me at all times. The guys there are a bunch of goof-offs and I don't like them to caddy for me. Even if I go into the clubhouse to have a drink and buy you a Coke, stay near. I'm afraid of what they might do if they get you alone."

My boss went golfing quite often, and I learned to be a good caddy. Geez, I was getting paid by the hour and spending half of the time enjoying the fresh air at the Sunnyside Country Club!

CHAPTER 24

Foundry Rats

A friend of mine named Roth asked me if I would like a job.

"I sure would, Roth!"

"It's hard work, but pays good money. My dad owns a small foundry, and he is casting Pineapple hand grenades for the Army. I know my dad will hire you, because you have transportation to work and back home late at night.

By the way, Tom, how is your Model A running?"

"Just fine," I said, "but it is hard as hell to get gasoline. I'm only allowed four gallons a week with the stamps in my ration card."

The foundry was on Mulberry Street, close to Black Hawk Creek. After school we went into the office and Roth introduced me to his dad. He told him I owned my own car, and that I also had work experience.

"Where have you previously worked, Tom?" he asked.

"I worked at the Flour City Box Factory all summer. You could call my boss there, if you want. I can give you his name."

"No need, Tom. If you worked at the box factory all summer, you must know how to work. You're hired," he said. "Roth, take Tom out and show him the ropes. We have a huge amount of castings poured, and they need tending to."

Roth showed me what to do, nothing complicated, just hard labor. Molten iron was poured in the sand molds all day. Our job, after school, was to take a hook, break up the molds, shake out the castings, load them into a wheelbarrow, haul them to another room, and then load them into the roller drum that smoothed off the burrs so they could be painted.

The foundry building was huge and half of it was rented out to the U.S. Government for storage. Why, no one could figure out, but thousands of sacks of wheat were stacked clear to the ceiling. What a combination: a foundry and wheat storage!

The wheat storage portion of the building was full of rats, and they had plenty to eat. When we were shaking out castings, sometimes a rat would get into the foundry and run down an aisle. The first worker to see it would holler, "Rat!" We would all look up and grab a shovel. As the rat ran down the aisle, one of us would hit it with the shovel, knock it out, pick the rat up by its tail, and throw it into the cupola. When its body hit the molten iron, it made a hissing noise and would immediately dissolve.

Then someone would yell, "Let them Japs get a little rat with their hand grenades!"

The foundry had an old-fashioned cupola. A steel pin was pulled and the bottom two doors would drop to empty the molten iron. A siren was blown when the pin was pulled to warn everyone to stay clear of the cupola. I had a wheelbarrow full of castings heading for the roller drums and the cupola was on my route. I heard screaming and yelling and instantly realized I was standing in front of the cupola and the pin had been pulled. Sometimes it would drop right away, and sometimes it would take a minute or two. The molten iron dropped to the floor just as I dived for the ground away from the cupola. Some workers doused me with a fire hose, and if I hadn't noticed the pin had been pulled and dived out of the way, I would have suffered severe damage to both legs. My only wound was on my right leg, and the scar is still there to this day.

One day, Roth said to me, "Tom, the government trucks parked out back have full tanks and no locks on them. One truck has started to drip gasoline on the ground. I have a piece of rubber hose and before we go home tonight, I'm going to treat you to a full tank of gas for your car."

After work, I pulled my Model A next to the truck leaking gasoline on the ground. Roth took off the gas cap, stuck in the hose, sucked on the end until gas started to flow, stuck the other end into my gas tank, and filled it up.

Roth said, "The gas has been running on the ground, so we might as well have it. You know, Tom, we're making hand grenades for the Army. They can furnish us some gas to get back and forth to work! My dad said he would tell the driver we drained the gasoline tank, because it was leaking on the ground and, if someone would throw down a cigarette, it could burn the whole foundry down. Besides, there is nothing he can do about it. My dad owns the building!"

CHAPTER 25

Showroom Showdown

One day in 1942 I was driving through downtown Waterloo and went past the Schukei Chevrolet Used Car Showroom. Schukei was located next to the Illinois Central Railroad tracks where a huge wooden water tank sat on wooden legs high enough to reach the water compartment of a train. The *Land of Corn* passenger train that traveled to Chicago always stopped there to fill its steam engine with water.

I drove around the block and parked my Model A right in front of Schukei's Showroom. I went inside and a salesman in a wrinkled suit and smoking a cigar met me at the door.

"What do you want, kid?" he snarled.

"I would like to look at that '34 Coupe I saw in the window and want to know the asking price," I said.

"You got a trade-in?"

I told him I did and that it was parked out front.

He looked out the window and asked, "What year Model A is that?"

"It's a 1929, sir," I answered. "Don't those yellow-spoke wheels look great?"

"I guess so. Let's go out and take a closer look."

We went outside, and he asked for the key to start it up.

"Set the spark and I will give the crank a turn," I said.

It started right up as always and the salesman pushed the gas pedal to the floor. He held it down until smoke started billowing out of the exhaust pipe and then let up completely and the four-cylinder engine made a little rattling noise from the abuse.

He handed me back the key and said gruffly, "Your Model A needs a lot of work, kid."

I said to the fat, cigar smoking, numbskull of a salesman, as calmly as I could, "Gosh, could I take a closer look at that nifty looking '34 Ford Coupe now?"

"Sure, kid, but your Model A needs an overhaul and we can't give you much for it."

We walked back into the showroom and I got in the '34 Coupe. All the keys were on a ring so I reached over, locked both doors, started up the engine, and pushed the pedal to the floor. It didn't take long before the room was filling with smoke, but I didn't let up. Mr. Speck, the used car manager, pounded on the window, but I still wouldn't let up. The fat, cigar smoking, salesman that always called me "kid" ran out the door and found Officer Duggan, the policeman on the west side beat. In the 1930's and '40's, a policeman walked a beat in the downtown area every day.

In stomped the salesman with Officer Duggan right behind. He saw all the smoke and said, "You need the Fire Department."

He then came over to the Coupe and tapped his billy club on the windshield.

I shut off the engine and got out of the car.

"What is going on, son?" he asked.

"See that salesman over there, sir?" I said as I pointed to him. "My Model A is parked out front and, well, he did the same thing to my car until it smoked and rattled. He could have damaged my engine, so I was only doing the same to see if their car smoked and rattled when I pushed it to the floor and then let up on the gas.

Officer Duggan said to the fat, wrinkled suit, cigar smoking, salesman, "Did you do that to his car?"

"I guess so, but I didn't hold down the gas pedal as long as the kid did."

"You dumb nut. You had it coming and I don't blame the kid for what he did."

I turned and looked back as I walked out of the showroom. Mr. Speck was chewing out the salesman or maybe firing him. That salesman thought he was dealing with a kid, but at fifteen, I had a legal driver's license and a good job as a telegrapher for the Illinois Central Railroad.

Later, I dealt with Mr. Speck when he was the new car manager. He remembered me and all the smoke in the showroom and said, "We never left all the keys in a car after you taught us that lesson!"

I guess he must have forgiven me!

CHAPTER 26

All Aboard

Around 1935 I lived on Fowler Street in Waterloo, Iowa, about ten blocks from the ICRR round house. There was a sharp curve in the tracks a few blocks from our home. When the steam engine blew the whistle, all the neighborhood kids grabbed a bucket and headed for the sharp curve in the tracks. Pieces of coal would always come flying off the engine at the curve. Sometimes I think the fireman shoveled off coal for us at that curve! I learned to fistfight at an early age to get my share of the coal from older kids. Back then, everyone heated their house with coal, and times were tough in America.

When I graduated from the ninth grade at Edison School, my mother said, "Where are you going to work, Tommy?"

I replied, "I am going to West Jr. with some of my friends." I enrolled at West Junior High and attended a class taught by the Illinois Central Railroad. I thought it would be a fun class and interesting to learn telegraphy. The teacher was a pleasant, retired ICRR Depot agent. Because I learned International Morse Code so quickly, I became the head of the class. The teacher also appreciated my superior handwriting. It was extremely important to write perfect railroad-style penmanship so there would be no mistakes in railroad train orders. I can still write in that style to this day.

I was fourteen years old and the only student the railroad hired. I was needed because all the young agents had been drafted into the army and the older ones needed some time off. A car would pick me up after school on Friday afternoon and drive me to a depot to work for the weekend. The railroad always found a place for me to stay and must have paid for my room and board. I really delighted in riding the steam engine back home to Waterloo on Sunday afternoon. The engineer said to me, "Hang on, Tom, when we hit a flying switch!"

I quit school and started to work full time when I turned fifteen. My assignment was the eastern division, which was from Waterloo to Dubuque, Iowa, and included the East Dubuque Tower in East Dubuque, Illinois. I operated the bridge owned by the ICRR that spans the Mississippi River in Dubuque.

Bridge spanning the Mississippi River in Dubuque, Iowa

CHAPTER 27

Masonville

Early in my career as a telegraph operator, the Illinois Central Railroad sent me to work in Masonville, Iowa. Although small, Masonville was a great railroad town and known as "the main line of mid-America." In 1995, I traveled through Masonville and the depot was still standing. I got out of my car and stared at the building and platform for a long time. It was to me a wonderful sight!

During the time I worked there, the railroad found me a place to stay in town. I was replacing a depot agent who had been drafted into the army and lived with his wife and two young daughters. I do not know how much she was paid, but I was always very well fed!

The depot was furnished with a table, four chairs, a desk for my telegraph equipment,

151

and a steel safe that held a loaded revolver. My instructions were to not touch the revolver even if the depot was robbed. "Let them have whatever they want and save yourself!"

I could see the platform and down the tracks through a large bay window. A few pictures adorned the wall and the floor was brick tile. The levers for the signal tower were in the corner towards the tracks. Outside were two flatbed carts used to load up baby chicks and miscellaneous goods sent through the Parcel Post. I received pay for anything I handled for the Parcel Post Company and for any Western Union telegraphs I sent.

The daily train from Waterloo, Iowa to Dubuque, Iowa and back always stopped and unloaded goods purchased by farmers and the townspeople. The conductor's name was Mr. Sullivan. He was a very kind man and always answered any of my questions. Mr. Sullivan endured one of the worst tragedies I could ever imagine. He lost all five of his sons on the same day in a Navy battle in the South Pacific.

The walls of his caboose were lined with posters of Hedy Lamar, Betty Grable, Lana Turner, and other 1940s movie stars. Mr. Sullivan said to me, "Tommy, you stay out of the caboose, because I'm afraid I would get in trouble if I let you see those pin-ups!" And you guessed it. When Mr.

Sullivan went into town for something, I looked inside the caboose. All the movie stars in the pin-ups were wearing full-length bathing suits! Times sure have changed.

One summer day, the dispatcher from Waterloo let me know tracks had washed out somewhere on the line and trains from the cities of New Orleans, San Francisco, and Los Angeles would be coming to Masonville. The three passenger trains could not be left on the main track, because a meat train was coming from Rath Packing Company in Waterloo. Meat trains had the right of way over all other trains, including passenger trains. All the cars were loaded with meat packed in ice and heading for the Armed Services. Because of the summer heat, water would pour out of the cars from the melting ice.

After I managed to get the passenger trains off the main line and onto the sidings, all three conductors came into the depot and were surprised to see such a young agent. They were dressed in their magnificent uniforms and it felt as though I had three kings in my depot! I introduced myself, and since it was noon, mustered up the courage to ask if they would like to have lunch with me. The woman I boarded with had just brought my lunch and always provided enough food to last all day. All three conductors sat down, we shared my lunch and had a good time visiting with one another while we.feasted on sandwiches made with fresh homemade bread and coffee. Later, the conductor of the New Orleans passenger train wrote to Mr. Johnson, President of the ICRR, about what a good job I did getting three passenger trains on and off the siding and that I had even shared my lunch with them. Mr. Johnson then wrote a letter to my mother and told her about the event and how competently I was handling the trains.

One day the dispatcher called to tell me we had an order for the meat train on its way. I told him I could already see the smoke, so the order had to be short. He started to dictate the order and it was a long one. As I wrote the order in railroad-style handwriting and read it back to him, I could hear the train coming. After an order was taken, it was folded up, put into a string loop and pulled closed. The string was then fastened on a Y-shaped wooden holder. As the train passed by, I would stand on the platform and hold the wooden holder with both arms toward the tracks. The fireman or brakeman would then stick out his arm and catch the message in the string. It was quite dangerous because you stood only a few feet from the engine. Usually I had plenty of time to get ready, but today I had not a minute to spare. In my rush, I forgot the platform was gravel and slid right into the engine. The meat trains had a huge engine and traveled at 100 miles per hour. The Y-shaped message stick hit the engine and knocked me down and back onto the platform. The train was stopped and the fireman and brakeman came running back to the platform. They were sure I had been killed. The ICRR always investigated any accident and it was determined to be the dispatcher's fault, not mine.

I enjoyed working at the Masonville depot, because there was always something happening… a lot of Parcel Posts and Western Union telegraphs. One week my paycheck was $75! I told my mother and she could hardly believe it. She worked at the Rath Packing Company in Waterloo and made $37.50 for six days of hard labor.

When I had to leave the Masonville depot, I said goodbye to the lady of the house and the two little girls. I almost cried. I had run the depot for nearly a year and it was hard to leave. The ICRR then sent me to Epworth, Iowa.

CHAPTER 28

Epworth

Epworth, Iowa, was a stop on the Illinois Central Railroad only because a Catholic Monastery located there. I was sent to Epworth because it had been raining pitchforks and hammer handles for days, and miles of track had washed out in the Epworth and Dubuque area. The ICRR found me a wonderful German couple to stay with on their farm. She was an excellent cook and even enticed me to like hot potato salad! I always helped milk the cows early in the morning before I went to work.

The depot was a small, ten-foot-by-ten-foot building housing one chair, a built-in desk, and a switchboard. Wasps had filled all the holes in the switchboard. I immediately hooked up my key and waited to hear from the dispatcher.

A monk from the monastery came to the door my first day and wanted telegrams sent to Chicago. Another monk had passed away and the family in Chicago needed to be notified. I made a nice amount of money that day sending and receiving telegrams.

One day I was sent a message that a work train was on its way from Alabama and someone was needed to take train orders. The Western Union telegraphers in Chicago used sidewinder keys and I could not copy that fast without a typewriter. I keyed them to slow down. That made them angry and they REALLY slowed down. The dispatcher in Waterloo let me know the train would be there in a few days. When it arrived, I found the overseer and told him I was available to take train orders for him when he needed to move the work train.

The railroad had an outhouse set up for me and gave me a set of pole climbing hooks. When the work train needed a work order to move, I would put the hooks on my shoes, climb up a telephone pole, clip on my key, and call the dispatcher in Waterloo. I would maybe climb a pole two or three times a day.

The work train had an engine, a caboose for the overseer, four sleeping cars, one cook-house car, and several flat cars that held tools and supplies including extra track, spikes, railroad ties, and anything needed to repair the track. The workers included fifty to seventy-five black men and about twenty black women who did the cooking and cleaning. They set up their own toilets and were very organized. When they spoke I couldn't understand what they were saying; the words sounded like some kind of gibberish to me, but it didn't really matter since they had been given orders to have no contact with me.

The overseer was a white man about 6′4″ tall. He wore leather pants, a loaded pistol, and had a leather whip about ten feet long wound up and hooked on his belt. One day I asked him how much the ICRR paid the workers. He said, "Nothing. The ICRR pays me, I furnish their food (which was mostly beans and corn bread) and then pay the workers what I think they are worth." When he was near, the men worked really hard. They drove spikes in pairs and would sing songs and never miss the spikes. It was a beautiful thing to see.

CHAPTER 29

East Dubuque

I had been on the job in Epworth only about two months when the dispatcher in Waterloo called to say I was being sent to the East Dubuque Tower in East Dubuque, Illinois, to train for two weeks. Then if the agent thought I could handle the job, I would take over the Tower.

Arriving in Dubuque was a little scary for me and worrying about my new assignment didn't help matters. The weather was very hot and the mayflies were so thick the snow plows were sent out to clear the streets. The railroad made arrangements for me to stay at a hotel in East Dubuque, Illinois, but because of its bad reputation for drinking and gambling, the ICRR kept me across the Mississippi River in Dubuque, Iowa.

The agent in charge of the Tower trained me for two weeks and never showed up for work the third week. I called the dispatcher in Waterloo and he told me, "Tommy, you are the new agent for the East Dubuque Tower. Congratulations!"

The inside of the tower had a single row of levers to move switches on the tracks and the lighted track layout was on the wall across from the switches. I had to leave the tower and go upstairs into another small building to open the middle section of the railroad bridge when tugboats needed to pass through. One morning I was watching the lighted track layout and a train was coming through the tunnel, its lights blinking along the board. I had received no message from the train on my key and, heaven forbid, another set of lights were blinking from the opposite direction. I had to make a split-second decision so I switched the track and ran one train into the ditch to prevent a head-on collision. It turned out to be the maintenance man on his four-wheel railroad cart, and in the ditch he went. He could have been killed, but was unhurt. The railroad did another investigation and determined it was not my fault. The maintenance man should not have been on the track or should have keyed me ahead of time.

Mr. Johnson, president of the railroad, called me and said, "Tommy, I have received only good reports about you. Keep up the excellent work. The accident was not your fault. You had to do what you did to prevent a head on collision."

Train Tunnel near Mississippi River Bridge

I really enjoyed running the Tower. Things were now going smoothly again and I enjoyed doing a lot of telegraphy work and helping trains make it safely across the bridge when a tugboat showed up, blew his whistle, and wanted me to open the middle section of the bridge for it to pass.

It had been raining for weeks; the river was high and rushing towards New Orleans. I went up into the bridge tower and pulled the controls to open the center section of the bridge for a

The author with his mother, Emma

barge. Unbelievably, the captain missed the opening and hit the bridge! It knocked a hole in the barge large enough to drive a car through. The bridge began to shimmy and shake. I called the dispatcher in Waterloo and told him what happened. He said, "Tommy, get off that bridge NOW!" He thought it was going to fall down so I ran out on the deck and jumped to the ground. You guessed it, another investigation.

My birthday was soon approaching and I traveled back to Waterloo to join the Navy. All my friends were going into the service and I thought it would be the thing to do. To join the service under the age of eighteen required the signature of a parent. My mother signed the consent form, I was enlisted on my seventeenth birthday, and sent to the Great Lakes Navy Training Center.

CHAPTER 30

NTSCH Radio School

The Great Lakes Navy Training Center. was located near Chicago on Lake Michigan.

My first hour there turned out to be a not very good beginning. Our bus full of recruits was taken to the cafeteria. where we all grabbed a tray and got in line. The servers kept loading up our plates, encouraging everyone to take more and more food. Some of the new recruits let them pile on enough for two or three men. I stopped the servers from giving me more food than I could eat, but it was still much more than I needed. A petty officer with a billy club came around, pounded his club on each table, and made all the recruits, including me, eat everything on his plate. I know that was the Navy's way of teaching us not to take more than we could eat and not to waste any food, but I was not used to such treatment.

I was at the Training Center a short time when we were given a test that included Morse code.

Not long after taking the test, the chief petty officer took me to his office and said, "Sailor, you're going to the University of Wisconsin to attend the Navy Training Radio School (NTSCH). Pack your belongings. You are leaving tomorrow, because a new class starts soon."

Wow! That sure was a surprise to me.

I boarded a bus and the Navy met me at the bus station and took me to my quarters on the campus of the University of Wisconsin. I was issued three new white uniforms and the Navy clerk asked if I needed new shoes. I said yes because the pair I received at the training center was too large. The clerk there just looked at my feet and threw me a pair of shoes. He didn't care if they fit or not.

The first hour at the NTSCH Radio School was just the opposite of the training school. We were treated well and I was even given a pair of shoes that fit my feet. My new barracks was a pleasant place on the campus of the University. A petty officer showed me to my room and assigned me a bed. The two other sailors in the room introduced themselves and filled me in on what was happening and what the rules were on campus. One of the sailors said the food was good here. That was music to my ears! I was

NTSCH Radio School, University of Wisconsin, Madison, Wisconsin

surprised to learn one of my roommates was from my hometown of Waterloo, Iowa.

Every Saturday we went off campus to Madison after barracks inspection. An officer would come and inspect everything in the dorm for cleanliness, including the bathroom. We also had to have our beds made up perfectly. If we did not pass inspection, there was no Saturday leave.

Well, the lazy galoot from Waterloo made us make his bed and do his share of the cleaning so we could pass inspection. We wanted to get off campus so badly that we put up with it. When I was discharged from the Navy a few years later, I found out the nitwit was working at the Waterloo Savings Bank as some kind of officer. I wanted to talk to the president of the bank about him, but decided to leave it alone. The first time I saw him at the bank, he turned his head and walked briskly away.

When we started classes I decided not to inform my superiors that I already knew Morse code. I just went along with what the teachers wanted me to do and learned their way of doing things. I became proficient enough that I could not write the code down fast enough with a pencil to keep up, so the instructor issued me a typewriter. Wow! Could I ever take down Morse code fast then!

We did not practice any words, just numbers and letters. I believe it was five letters and then five numbers, all coded. Every ship at sea had a telegrapher that wrote or typed the letters down, hour after hour. The captains of all the ships had a way to decode the five groups of letters and then could tell if any of the messages were for their ship. A telegrapher might type the code for months and none of it was for his ship. I bet the Japs went crazy trying to make sense out of those jumbled letters!

Most ships had three or four telegraphers, but we were all taught how to copy code for several hours and how to lay on a hard surface to get some rest in a short period of time. In case some of the telegraphers became sick or were killed in a battle at sea, we had to be ready to fill in for them.

An officer came onto the classroom one day and gave a talk about copying groups of letters that did not make any sense over and over for hours and how it could affect our brain. He told us we might have a problem with bad dreams and, if that happens, to come to his office and talk with him about it. I found out later he was a shrink.

I didn't think it would happen, but it did eventually affect me. After weeks of taking code over and over and over that didn't make any sense, I started to have bad dreams. I would go to bed and dream the same dream every night. As soon as I got to sleep, a stagecoach pulled by several horses would race down a tunnel, and I had to run ahead of it or be run over. That darn stagecoach chased me all night and, finally after a few weeks, I had had it and decided to make an appointment to go see the shrink. He said, "Sailor, we can fix that problem easily. When you go to bed tonight, think of a way to stop the stagecoach from chasing you."

That night I started to have the same dream. I was in the tunnel and could hear the horses coming, so I heated up a huge kettle of tar and had a box of feathers nearby. The coach came racing down the tunnel and I tarred and feathered it. I never had that dream again! Later, the shrink asked me how I came out and I told him about my solution.

"Good for you, sailor!" he said.

We began to have exercise classes taught by the same officer who showed us how to get some sleep on a table or floor. The campus was on Lake Mendota, so the Navy furnished us with a very large rowboat and several sets of oars. He would take us out into the lake and we would row for about an hour. It was really good exercise!

One day we were out rowing when some of the crew got their oars tangled up and we all started laughing. That was the wrong thing to do. He made us row back and tie the boat to the dock with a line. Then we had to row tied to the

dock and, yes, nobody did any laughing after that workout!

I learned the college had a dating service and decided to try it out. I had my date meet me the next Saturday afternoon at the office around 4:00 PM. She arrived on time and was a really nice looking girl. One problem, though. I was seventeen years old and she was twenty. We went to eat at a restaurant near the lake, walked around downtown for a while, and then I took her back to the dating service office. She thanked me for the dinner and was very nice to me, but I felt like she was old enough to be my sister! I never used the dating service again.

Everything at the telegraph school was going well. An instructor told me I was at the head of the class and, when we graduate, I would be appointed to a Third Class Petty Officer.

"Will I get a raise in pay?" I asked.

He laughed and said, "Not much, Tom."

Unfortunately, the instructor informed me just before graduation that, because the war would end soon, the Navy was not giving anyone the rank above Seaman First Class. I sure was disappointed, because I was looking forward to a little more pay than twenty-five dollars a month.

The Navy had a very nice graduation ceremony for us. They furnished a keg of beer and all kinds of good food. The class was all seated, and most of graduates had parents attending, so the room was almost full. An officer came out on stage to speak.

He stepped up to the mike and said, "I want Seaman First Class Tom Shepherd to please stand up."

Wow, that scared me a little, but I stood up.

"We have plenty of beer for everyone except Seaman First Class Tom Shepherd, because in the state of Wisconsin the legal drinking age is eighteen and this Seaman First Class is only seventeen."

Everyone laughed! I think I had a couple glasses of beer anyway.

CHAPTER 31

Philippines

At the age of eighteen, I was serving in the United States Navy during World War II. The wisdom teeth on both sides of my mouth started breaking through the skin and, holy cow, did it hurt! I was stationed in a small town called Guiuan on the island of Samar in the Philippines. The U.S. Seabees were building a tent hospital on the island and the dentist on the new base also had a small tent for an office. I was told to go see the dentist where his tent was located.

As I opened the flap to his tent, he said, "What's the matter with you, sailor?"

"Sir, my wisdom teeth are coming through and, wow, it sure hurts."

He took a look and said, "They need to come out, but I don't have any pain killer. All

177

the painkillers the navy had were used up in the Battle of Okinawa. Take this shot of whiskey. Maybe that will help a little."

I sat down in a chair and he pulled out my wisdom teeth, one on each side of my mouth. I thought my eyes were coming out along with them!

I spit out a lot of blood and the dentist said, "I want you to go over to the hospital tent and report to the head doctor. You need to be watched at least through the night."

I walked to the hospital and found the head doctor. I told him the dentist had just pulled my wisdom teeth and that I was to report here because he felt I needed to be looked after for the night.

The doctor said, "You look all right to me, sailor." Then he yelled, "Nurse, put this sailor to work."

The hospital tents were filled with sick and wounded soldiers and marines. The nurse said, "Come with me, sailor. We need help carrying the wounded and setting up army cots."

I worked all night, but when morning came, I took off for navy headquarters and reported for duty.

My assigned job was to be a courier for the army and navy. I was issued a leather pouch with a wide shoulder strap and a 45-caliber revolver side arm. I delivered sealed messages to the army who had landed on the island of Samar three days before General MacArthur had landed on the island of Leyte, and the base on Leyte needed to communicate with the navy base near Guiuan. An LCI (Landing Craft Infantry) went from Guiuan down the coast to Suluan and back every day. The Seabees had built benches on the LCI for any military personnel passengers. Whenever I boarded the LCI for the trips to Suluan, there were from five to ten communist soldiers also aboard. Each soldier carried a machine gun with a heavy wire stock that folded over the gun and a leather strap for carrying it. They always stared at me, knowing I was carrying sealed orders in my leather pouch and that made me nervous. Maybe the loaded 45-caliber pistol I wore on my belt made them nervous too!

The LCI had a crew of six sailors, including the captain and a really good cook. They always invited me to have lunch with them. I guess I was worried about where and when my next good meal was going to be!

One day I mentioned to the captain that I felt uneasy sitting with the Communist soldiers, because they all carried loaded machine guns.

The captain said, "I don't blame you, but we have to put up with it for now. The government is letting them roam the Philippines because they help fight the Japanese army."

After a few months, I didn't see them any longer so I asked the captain of the LCI what happened to them.

"There was some kind of disagreement with the Pilipino army and the Communist soldiers all disappeared into the jungle. I guess you could say they all went underground."

On one of my trips down the Coast of Calicoan Island, we had a delay leaving the island of Suluan because of high winds and rough waves. Finally, the storm let up some so the captain decided to take off and we returned late at night. I usually walked back to Guiuan. It was well over a mile, but there was a short cut through the jungle. I had taken it once before in the daytime and, since I was tired and eager to get back to my barracks, I decided to take it this night. The trail was about three feet wide and, because of the dense jungle, was like going through a tunnel. I was walking as fast as I could and coming from the opposite direction was a water buffalo. He must have heard or smelled me, because he had lowered his head and I walked right smack into him. It surprised both of us! He raised his head up and I landed between his giant horns. I went flying and then dove into the jungle, and he took off running.

Shortly after the Communist army went underground, the U.S. Navy discontinued my courier job and sent me to work in the post office. The Seabees had just finished building the post office and were handling all the mail for the navy and marines in the South Pacific. My new job was easy work. All packages traveled down a conveyor and my job was to pick them up, slowly tip them back and forth near my ear, and listen for a gurgle. Mothers and wives were sending pints of whiskey in loaves of bread or anything to hide the bottles and keep from getting busted. It was illegal to send alcoholic beverages through the U.S. mail and the navy tried their best to obey the law. I hated that part of my job, because I could detect every pint. I only set aside half of the alcohol I found and let the rest go through. I wanted to let all of them go through, but I was afraid I would get in trouble with my superiors. The U.S. Navy officer in charge took all the pints set aside each day. I bet the officer's compound had plenty to drink in their bar!

While working at the post office, we lived in tents close by. We had to make sure each of the tent flaps were tied down when we left for work, because monkeys would sneak into the tents and tear everything apart looking for food. It did no good to shoot them, because they were everywhere. We quickly learned our lesson and decided to make our tent monkey-proof. We received a beer ration, but I didn't like beer so I would give mine away. One of the sailors in my tent had a small tin plate that he would pour a little beer into and set on the ground near our tent. After the monkeys came down from the trees and lapped up the beer, they could hardly walk and would try to hang by their tails, but were so drunk they would fall.

It didn't take the Seabees long and they had the tropical Quonset huts erected. Twenty sailors were assigned to each hut and ours was built on an especially high hill. The huts were made of metal with plywood floors, and when raining, it sounded like you were standing in a tin can.

The sailors in our hut had all different types of jobs. Some were postal workers, hospital workers, office workers, and one was a truck driver. We loved the truck driver! He wasn't afraid to steal anything he could get into his truck. He was hauling lumber and dropped off enough two-by-fours for us to build bed frames. He also managed to get twenty mattresses! If he was hauling food for the Mess Hall, he would give us cases of canned goods or a case of eggs. He dropped off two camp stoves and anything he thought we could use. The base was growing fast and the lines at the Mess Hall were getting longer and longer, so we prepared our own food when we had it. Our truck driver even brought us enough materials to build a screened porch onto the rear of the hut. The hospital workers brought us ice and a Pilipino woman picked up our laundry and cleaned and pressed our uniforms. We had it made!

The first time I went to the mess hall to eat, I sure had a surprise. The menu was Navy beans, bread, cold coffee, and scrambled eggs. The eggs were green instead of yellow and smelled funny. I later learned that when the eggs were cracked open and put in a frying pan, the yolk and white would mix together and turn green. I thought it was nice of the cooks to put caraway seeds in the bread until I found out it was some kind of weevil. The cooks were not going to take the time to sift them out, but you couldn't taste them so I ate the bread anyway.

Once when a friend and I were standing in a long line waiting to get some chow, a black sailor held up a carton of Lucky Strike cigarettes and was bragging about how he got them. One carton of Lucky Strikes was worth more than ten cartons of Old Gold cigarettes. The Navy would give you all the Old Golds you wanted, but Lucky Strikes were rare. A sailor from the South picked up a two-by-four from a pile of leftover lumber and hit the black sailor on the head.

I yelled to my friend, "Let's get out of here!"

We took off running and it was a good thing we did. It turned into a race riot and several white and black sailors were injured. That was the end of going to the mess hall for us!

The Philippine Islands were infested with rats and they soon discovered our hut. At night, a sailor at the end of the hut would reach up with a stick to turn off the light, and the hut would fill with rats running everywhere. I nailed a funnel-shaped tin around each leg of my bed so they couldn't climb up, but I still woke up twice with a rat on my chest. Some of the sailors in our hut put a pail of water by their bed, tied a candy bar on a string just out of reach of the rats, and ran a board up to the top of the pail. When a rat scurried up the ramp and reached for the candy bar, the sailor hit it over the head. It was a terrible mess. Finally, the navy came with a truck loaded with used, crank case oil from the airport and covered the plywood floor. It was thought that would keep the rats out, but it didn't work. The rats even seemed to like the oil. Then the navy decided to put a mongoose in each hut. The mongoose would kill a rat and then suck out the blood. He had plenty of rats to kill, but it was a disgusting sight. It helped a little, but the mongoose was a horrible little animal.

One evening a group of us were out in our screened porch relaxing and having a beer. Our mongoose had just killed a rat and was in a corner sucking out its blood.

One of the guys pulled out his revolver and yelled, "I can't take this anymore" and shot the mongoose. The bullet knocked out the corner post and the roof fell down, but it was the rats or the mongoose. We decided to put up with the rats.

In September 1945, the U.S. Navy had an entire fleet of battleships, cruisers, and aircraft carriers anchored off the island of Samar. We were told they would be sailed around the world to show the U.S. Navy still had a powerful fleet of ships. Sailors were needed so I signed up. I thought it would be interesting to sail around the world. The next day all of the personnel at the navy base were gathered together and loaded into trucks. We were taken to a mountainous area somewhere on the island of Samar and put in an enormous cave. After we were all settled, we learned why. A typhoon was approaching the island and we would be in severe danger on lower ground. The naval fleet could not stay anchored near the island, so all the ships set sail for the Pacific Ocean. They headed straight into the typhoon, but never lost a ship. The fleet never returned to Samar, so there went my trip around the world!

Church in the Philippines

The typhoon hit the island and destroyed most of the naval base. When we returned from the cave, I could hardly believe my eyes! The post office was completely gone. The storm must have destroyed the building and washed it out to sea. We hurried to see if our Quonset hut was still standing. It was on a hill about a mile from the ocean and was spared. I wondered about the town of Guiuan, but it appeared to have been spared. The Catholic Church, the oldest on the island, was made of stone and I supposed it had survived a good many typhoons. The local people were busy repairing their straw huts, although the grass roofs had stood up to the winds remarkably well.

The typhoon changed a lot of things for me. I now had no steady job, so I reported to Headquarters every morning. Many lost their jobs because of the typhoon and it was difficult for the Navy to find new jobs for all the sailors now out of work. One day ten of us were sent to the officer's mess hall to peel potatoes. The cook showed us the potatoes and we asked what time we needed to be finished.

He said, "Around ten o'clock would be OK."

We played cards and did everything we could think of to kill time. At 9:45 we started peeling potatoes and finished before ten o'clock.

One morning a jeep came and picked up two of us sailors and we were taken to the naval airport on Samar. We loaded up as many boxes as we could get on the jeep and went out to the landing strip to repair holes. Our job was to open the boxes, unwrap aviator watches, and throw them in the holes. After we worked all day, a crew would put a little asphalt on each hole and pound it flat. I asked if I could keep a watch, even though I knew it wouldn't be allowed.

The officer in charge said, "The U.S. Government made a deal with the watchmakers that no watches would be brought back to the States, because then no servicemen would buy watches when they returned home."

Another job I did kept me busy for a few weeks and was quite enjoyable. We loaded jeeps on an LCI, took them out in the Pacific Ocean, and pushed them overboard.

After that, I was assigned to a job driving trucks into a swamp in the jungle until they were stuck in the mud. That was a lot of fun! As soon as we buried the trucks deep in the swamp, a marine with a BAR (Browning Automatic Rifle) shot out the tires and engines. Some of the trucks and jeeps were brand new.

We asked a chief petty officer, "Why are we destroying all of these jeeps and trucks?"

"The U.S. Government tried to sell them to the Philippine government, but they wanted them for free, so the admiral gave an order to destroy them."

A friend of mine from South Dakota told me a sign had been posted at Headquarters to explain a new point system. If a soldier had enough points, he could ship home.

"Wow! Let's go check it out!" I said.

A soldier was awarded points for serving overseas, points for being in the Reserves, and points for other criteria. I had enough to go home! After entering the office, I told the clerk my name and serial number. He looked up the information and confirmed that I had enough points. He wrote all the necessary information on the form when I noticed he had misspelled my last name.

I said, "Sir, there are a lot of ways to spell Shepherd, but you have spelled mine wrong."

"Are you telling me I can't spell, sailor? Get the hell out of here."

When my name came up to go home and was posted on the bulletin board, it was still misspelled, which caused some confusion when it was time to send my records back home. I was assigned to a ship heading to the States and on the second day at sea, the captain told us we could shoot off all the guns until the ammunition was depleted. It was fun shooting at sailfish and anything else we could see in the water.

When we were about two days from San Francisco, the captain had us dismantle the guns as best we could and throw them all overboard. We completely stripped the ship, including the radio equipment. Everything we could unbolt went overboard. The ship had already been sold for scrap.

We made good time sailing home. I believe it took less than a week. When I went to the South Pacific on the *General William Mitchell*, we zigzagged all the way so a Japanese submarine would have a difficult time shooting a torpedo at the ship. It cost a lot of time and took us thirty-two days to reach the Philippines.

Today was a peach of a day, no clouds, no wind, and the Pacific Ocean was calm. With binoculars, we could see the Golden Gate Bridge and when we saw that bridge our whole life changed. We were going to land soon on the good old United States of America! Now the navy food would become palatable and we would maybe even get dessert. As soon as we landed, I was taken to the naval base on Treasure Island and reported to an officer in the ready room. We discussed my situation, but I could not get a discharge.

The officer said, "I will do everything I can to find your lost records, sailor. In the mean time, I am assigning you to duty on a Chris Craft Cruiser that needs another crew member." Boy, was I disappointed!

Grandma Friedrichs

A letter from the author to his grandmother:

Dearest Grandma,

It is Thursday night as I set in my hut writing to you. It rained most of the day, but is terrible hot now. I received a lovely birthday card you sent me, yesterday. Thanks a million.

I am just fine and eating and sleeping good. The chow is nothing like we got in the States for it is all canned and de-hydrated. We sleep on Army cots which I think are very comfortable. Our recreation is a movie every nite and sometimes a ball game during the day.

The Philipinos run around here all day selling all kinds of stuff for about ten prices more than it should be. They sell grass skirts and bolo knives mostly.

The islands here are all jungle with coconut trees and all the trimmings. They are kind of pretty in a way, but nothing like good old Iowa. We have a huge fleet out in the bay and the little Philipino canoes sure look funny beside them. The Philipinos are all strong Catholics, especially the girls.

I am waiting to go aboard a ship any day now,,maybe before you receive this letter. I came out here on a huge transport that carried 5000 of us, not including a 500 man crew.

I sure would like to be home for Christmas, but I doubt if I will make it. I would like to see China, Japan, and a few of those places first.

Well, I will sign off for now. It is getting close for taps to sound.

All my Love,
Your Grandson, Tom

THOMAS J. SHEPHERD S℞ (RM)
322-47-14
R/S NAVY 3149
C/O F.P.O. SAN FRANCISCO, CALIF

MRS. HELEN FREDRICKS
ELGIN, IOWA
U.S.A.

Via Air Mail

CHAPTER 32

Treasure Island

What a wonderful day it was when we arrived in San Francisco and our ship sailed under the Golden Gate Bridge! We knew we were finally home. I was sent to the naval base on Treasure Island and reported to the commanding officer as soon as I arrived. He really didn't know what to do with me, because, since all of my records had been lost, I had no proof I was a member of the U.S. Navy.

After assigning me to a barracks, the officer in charge said, "We are going to try everything we can to find your records. In the meantime, I am sending you to duty on a powerboat that needs another crewmember. Since you are a seaman first class, you will have a seaman under your rank and a petty officer third class over your rank, so he will be in charge."

Our duty was to drive a boat out into the bay to the anchored naval ships and bring back officers who were starting shore leave.

The next morning I walked down to the dock where the boat was anchored to get acquainted with the other crew members. I could hardly believe my eyes!

The third class petty officer shook my hand and said, "Ain't she a beauty!"

Anchored at the dock was a thirty-two-foot Chris Craft Cruiser. The mahogany hull was varnished and had clean, white painted trim.

The officer said, "She has a powerful engine. Come on guys. Let's go fill her up, take her out, and see what she can do!"

We got out of sight of Treasure Island and opened her up. With all that power, I thought we were flying! The petty officer was quite reckless. When we got too close to shore, we hit some rocks, but fortunately there was no damage to the boat.

Almost under the Golden Gate Bridge was a dock to tie up the boat and a tavern where we ate fish cooked in corn meal, shoe string potatoes, and drank beer every day. I thought we spent too much time at the Blue Moon Tavern, but I was not in charge, so I just did what I was told.

The cruiser had some modifications done to accommodate sixteen officers at a time. There were seats for eight on each side and plenty of room for the three of us in the cabin. If the bay was rough, the petty officer would rock the boat a little, seawater came over the sides, and the officers would get a bit wet. None of them complained and the petty officer thought it was fun.

We had to make many runs with the boat loaded with officers on Saturday and Sunday, but during the week things were slow, so we were able to just do as we pleased.

One day a storm was forecasted to blow into the bay area, and we were heading for our dock. The waves were already getting rough and bouncing us around rather hard. As we passed a merchant marine ship, the captain signaled us to come close to his ship. He had heard about the approaching storm and wanted us to take a line from his ship and tie it to a nearby buoy.

I yelled to the petty officer, "No way! Don't do it! It's too dangerous."

He ignored my advice and yelled to the captain to throw a mooring line down to us.

I said again, "That merchant marine ship is not part of the U.S. Navy and, besides, the storm is getting worse."

The captain ordered his seamen to throw down a line, and so now we were committed to do it. We tied the line to our boat and started toward the closest buoy. The strong winds pushed us back toward the line, and it became tangled around our propeller. It killed the engine, and the storm pushed us into the side of the ship. We were in a terrible predicament.

The petty officer said, "One of us will have to go down behind the boat and cut us loose, so we'll need a knife. Just pray that the engine will start again or we'll really be in trouble!"

A seaman offered his pocketknife. It had a long, sharp blade and was our only hope.

"I'll go overboard and try to cut us loose," I volunteered.

"OK, Tom. Let's tie a line around your waist. If you get in the undercurrent, you could be pulled under and drown. We will keep the line taut and if you jerk on it, we can help you back up to the boat."

I opened the knife, put it between my teeth, took off my life vest, and inhaled a deep breath of air. Sliding off the rear of the boat and into the water, I pushed myself as hard and as quickly as I could to reach the propeller. Fortunately, the line wasn't wound around the shaft as tightly as we thought. I cut off the line to the merchant marine ship, pushed myself away from the propeller, and then jerked the rope tied around my waist to signal the crew to pull me up. Our boat was now free, but I was still in great danger if we crashed back against the ship. It could knock me off and it would be almost impossible for me to get back into the boat, but the crew grabbed my arms and pulled me up. When I was safe in the boat, the Petty Officer turned the key, and the engine started. We all yelled and screamed at our good luck. He pulled the throttle wide open and we headed for our dock, crashing through gigantic waves as we went. We made it back safely and tied up the boat with extra lines because of the storm.

After securing the boat, we went back to our quarters and learned from the OD (Officer of the Day) that we all had shore leave the coming weekend. The petty officer said, "What a break! Let's all go out and celebrate our good luck getting free from the merchant ship."

We talked about our experience and I said apologetically, "As soon as I cut us loose, the tension on the mooring line must have been released and the propeller was able to turn again. I'm sorry, seaman, but I couldn't take time to close the knife, so I had to just let it drop. I really didn't think I would get back to the boat before I ran out of air."

When our shore leave began, we all put on our dress uniforms. I had purchased a uniform from a sailor who needed a little cash. He had recently had it hand-made in Hong Kong by expert Chinese tailors when his ship was docked there. The outside of the suit was regulation, but the inside was not since it was lined with silk. All the silk was embroidered with ships and beautiful ocean scenes. I wasn't afraid to wear it passing the marines at the gates, because they could not see any of the lining. If they found out it was made in Hong Kong, they would make me take it off and probably punch holes in it.

The marine guards were experts in detecting pints of liquor any sailor tried to sneak onto the base. They would break them up with billy clubs and make the sailor walk back to his quarters with broken glass and whiskey running down his legs. I saw that happen with my own eyes.

The three of us left our base around noon. I had a little trouble leaving, because of my temporary I.D. card. The marine on duty had never seen a temporary I.D.

He looked at it and said, "Stand right here, sailor. I have to show this I.D. to my superior."

He returned in a few minutes, handed back my I.D., and pointed to the gate. I took off running and caught up with my friends. We boarded a bus that took us to downtown Oakland. The petty officer had a favorite tavern in the downtown area, where we went as soon as we got off the bus. The petty officer knew the bartender, so he told him the story about our getting tied up to the merchant marine ship and how we got loose.

The bartender came over to me and said, "What do you want to drink, sailor? It's on the house."

I pointed and said, "I'll have whatever the officer is drinking."

He set the drink in front of me and I picked up the glass and took a sip. It wasn't bad, so I had another and another, until I couldn't see the bartender or the shelves of liquor behind the bar. I had never drunk any booze like that in my entire life and had a complete blackout! I had no idea where my friends went, where I was, or what happened to me. When I came to, I was in a navy vehicle of some sort with a canvas top. It looked just like a British Land Rover, but the Land Rover would not be built until around 1950. The driver was a young lady wearing a navy military uniform and was an officer of some kind.

She said to me, "Tom, are you coming to?"

"What happened to me? You know my name?"

"Yes, Tom. Let me refresh your memory a little. Do you remember when we were on the train going across the country? We were in the same passenger car and the rusty windows would not close completely. It was cold, so we huddled together at night trying to keep warm. You were concerned about sleeping next to an officer and I told you, 'It's OK, Tom. I will see to it that nothing happens.' I sure enjoyed your company on that train ride."

"I remember the train ride to California, but how did I get in this vehicle with you now?"

The lady officer continued, "Don't worry about that. You foolishly drank so much alcohol, we thought you were going to die. I'm happy to see you are recovering."

"Where are we going?" I asked.

"I wasn't sure where to go when I first picked you up. You were so sick, I thought of taking you to the naval base hospital. Your two friends helped me lift you into my vehicle and you seemed to respond a little, so I decided you would be OK, and I was right. I'm taking you back to your base on Treasure Island, but before I do, we are taking a drive up into the mountains to show you where I spend a lot of my time. I don't want to let you off at the base still a little drunk or you might get into trouble. It will be Sunday morning by the time we arrive at the base and you should feel a lot better by then. Look out of the window, Tom. What do you see?"

"Holy cow! I can see all of San Francisco! It's beautiful! Where are we going?" I asked again.

"We've been climbing this narrow road for a long

time and it's pitch black outside. How can you see where you are going?"

"Quit worrying, Tom. I know where I'm going and have driven this road many times."

We continued to climb when the road turned sharply, and it was obvious we had reached our destination. There stood a magnificent brick and stone house ... no, castle ... several stories high and reaching almost to the clouds. The scene took my breath away.

"Is this a dream?"

She said, "This is no dream. This is where I live most of the time. Isn't it a dream-come-true?"

Then we turned around and headed back down the mountain road. We arrived at the base Sunday morning just as it began to get light.

"I have to go now, Tom," she said, "and you had better get back to your barracks and sleep. We had an unbelievably good time last night, but you were out of it half of the time and probably won't remember much. You will see me again sometime in the years to come, but I will not be able to talk with you. I will wave, and someday we will be together again. I promise. Tom, I am your guardian angel."

"What is your name?" I asked.

"You do not need to know my name, Tom. All you need to know is I am with you when you need me. Go to your barracks now and get some sleep."

I took her advice, got into bed, and slept for several hours. When I woke up, I felt sick and had a terrible headache. I thought about my guardian angel and, of course, dismissed it all as a dream.

When I woke up Sunday morning, the OD told me I was to report to headquarters. As soon as I walked through the door, the naval officer said, "Sailor, we found your records and you are going to Shoemaker, California, for separation from the U.S. Navy."

I received an honorable discharge and was awarded four medals: Asiatic Pacific, American Arena, Victory, and the Philippine Liberation. I didn't care much about the medals, but I was also given $321.65 and $100.90 for a travel allowance. When the officer handed me the check, I jumped to attention, saluted the officer, and said, "322-47-14, sir."

That was the last time I ever saluted an officer and gave my serial number!

Sixty years later, my wife and I were driving along the California coast on Highway One and stopped in Santa Barbara to see the sights. One of the attractions was a pier about two hundred feet wide that extended out into the harbor for a quarter of a mile. Steel stairs, for sitting and enjoying the view, stretched down to the water, and a raft-like structure had been built for the sea lions to climb up on and sun themselves. I walked down the steps and when I reached the observation platform, spotted a huge sea lion. He stared at me, and I stared back. I felt as though I had seen him somewhere before. As he looked into my eyes, my mind seemed to say to me, "Go up the stairs." I quickly climbed the stairs onto the pier and froze in my tracks. On the other side of the pier stood my guardian angel! She was still young and dressed in her navy officer's uniform. She waved at me as she had told me she would so many years before, got into the Land Rover, and drove off.

I was so startled, I couldn't move! Many of the things I believe happened could have been a dream, but three things absolutely happened and were not a dream: Our train ride together from Chicago to San Francisco, my angel picking me up and taking care of me when I was dead drunk in Oakland, and my angel showing herself to me after sixty years and waving to me as she had predicted.

Epilogue

All the events in this book were experienced as I grew from childhood to a young man in Waterloo, Iowa, during the Great Depression and World War II. It was delightful to look back and relive my adventures of trying to get rich with a homemade diving helmet made from an old sidearm heater, sneaking through fences at the Clyde Miller Rodeo and taking a chance at getting whipped by a cowboy, keeping calm during the landing of a disabled army spotter plane in a watermelon patch and working for the Illinois Central Railroad at the age of fifteen during the steam engine era.

If you are a senior reader, most likely you can relate to the Great Depression era memories. Holy cow! How about pig tails and dandelion greens, dusting mold off of dried orange rinds for a treat, our mothers smearing goose grease on our chests as a remedy for colds and sore throats, the perfect balanced stealy, carrying a jackknife in our pocket, keeping that 1929 Model A running, and learning to box like Joe Lewis?

Perhaps you have some of the same memories I have about my childhood, and, jiminy crickets, maybe they gave your heart a tug to read about them.

About the Author

Tom Shepherd was born October 6, 1927 in Waterloo, Iowa. He attended telegraphy classes at West Junior High and was employed by the Illinois Central Railroad at the age of fourteen. On his seventeenth birthday, Tom enlisted in the U.S. Navy and was able to use his telegraph skills for Uncle Sam.

Tom joined the Waterloo Fire Department July 1, 1950, and retired as Captain after thirty-two years of service. During his time with the fire department, he expanded on the entrepreneurial skills of his youth by starting his own construction business, a real estate company, and an appraisal company.

He now spends his summers in Spirit Lake, Iowa, and winters in Mesa, Arizona. He enjoys grilling, driving his jeep, country music, and writing.